THE TWELVE GIFTS of LIFE RECOVERY®

Stephen Arterburn | David Stoop

THE TWELVE GIFTS

GIFTS

OF LIFE RECOVERY®

TYNDALE®
MOMENTUM

An Imprint of
Tyndale House Publishers, Inc.

Visit Tyndale Momentum online at www.tyndalemomentum.com.

The Twelve Gifts of Life Recovery: God's Hope and Strength for Your Journey

Designed by Stephen Vosloo

Published in association with the literary agency of Alive Literary Agency, 7680 Goddard Street, Suite 200, Colorado Springs, CO 80920, www .aliveliterary.com.

Library of Congress Cataloging-in-Publication Data

Arterburn, Stephen, date.
  The twelve gifts of life recovery : hope for your journey / Stephen Arterburn, David Stoop.
    pages cm
  Includes bibliographical references.
  ISBN 978-1-4964-0269-1 (sc)
1. Twelve-step programs—Religious aspects—Christianity.   2. Gifts—Religious aspects—Christianity.   I. Title.
  BV4596.T88A826 2015
  248.8'629—dc23   2015011978

Printed in the United States of America

21	20	19	18	17	16	15
7	6	5	4	3	2	1

Table of Contents

The Twelve Steps of Alcoholics Anonymous

1. We admitted we were powerless over alcohol—
   that our lives had become unmanageable.

2. Came to believe that a Power greater than
   ourselves could restore us to sanity.

3. Made a decision to turn our will and our lives
   over to the care of God *as we understood Him.*

4. Made a searching and fearless moral inventory
   of ourselves.

5. Admitted to God, to ourselves, and to another
   human being the exact nature of our wrongs.

6. Were entirely ready to have God remove all these
   defects of character.

7. Humbly asked Him to remove our shortcomings.

8. Made a list of all persons we had harmed, and
   became willing to make amends to them all.

9. Made direct amends to such people wherever possible, except when to do so would injure them or others.

10. Continued to take personal inventory and when we were wrong promptly admitted it.

11. Sought through prayer and meditation to improve our conscious contact with God, *as we understood Him*, praying only for knowledge of His will for us and the power to carry that out.

12. Having had a spiritual awakening as the result of these Steps, we tried to carry this message to alcoholics, and to practice these principles in all our affairs.

The Twelve Steps of Life Recovery

1. We admitted we were powerless over our problems and that our lives had become unmanageable.

2. We came to believe that a Power greater than ourselves could restore us to sanity.

3. We made a decision to turn our wills and our lives over to the care of God.

4. We made a searching and fearless moral inventory of ourselves.

5. We admitted to God, to ourselves, and to another human being the exact nature of our wrongs.

6. We were entirely ready to have God remove all these defects of character.

7. We humbly asked God to remove our shortcomings.

8. We made a list of all persons we had harmed and became willing to make amends to them all.

9. We made direct amends to such people wherever possible, except when to do so would injure them or others.

10. We continued to take personal inventory, and when we were wrong, promptly admitted it.

11. We sought through prayer and meditation to improve our conscious contact with God, praying only for knowledge of his will for us and the power to carry it out.

12. Having had a spiritual awakening as the result of these Steps, we tried to carry this message to others, and to practice these principles in all our affairs.

The Twelve Steps used in *The Twelve Gifts of Life Recovery* have been adapted with permission from the Twelve Steps of Alcoholics Anonymous.

Introduction

CONGRATULATIONS ON YOUR RECOVERY!

Okay, maybe you're in the very early stages, having only recently admitted that you are powerless over your problems and that your life has become unmanageable; or maybe you've been working the Twelve Steps of Life Recovery for months, years, or even decades. Either way, the fact that you are on the journey toward recovering your life as it was meant to be lived is cause for celebration. You're moving in the right direction, and we encourage you to keep going.

We have chosen the language of celebration intentionally because, in a sense, that's what this book is all about. And as with any good celebration, there are some gifts to be unwrapped along the way. We're calling them the twelve gifts of life recovery.

The life recovery process will take you far beyond

the day-to-day struggle of a problem-focused life and will teach you new ways of living. As you continue along the path to recovery, you will begin to experience a life that is rich and full; a life that goes far beyond simply getting free from your problem behaviors. Yes, you will gain victory in the areas where you have struggled, but you will also find that life recovery touches your *entire* life.

As you persist in the journey of life recovery, God will give you gifts—or blessings—from time to time to strengthen and encourage you. Because they are gifts, you can't earn them; and because they can come to you at any time, you might not always realize when a gift has fallen in your lap. That's why we've written this book. We want you to recognize the gifts so you can celebrate them when they arrive.

Think of these gifts as some of the natural fruits of the recovery process. As you repair the damage you have caused in your own life and in the lives of others because of your problems, you will begin to discover *hope, power, character, clarity, security, abundance, wisdom, self-control, courage, happiness, serenity,* and *peace.* These are not automatic results of "working the program"—they are *gifts* that may come to us along the way—but by working the program we prepare ourselves to receive the gifts and to know what to do with them.

So as you keep working your life recovery program, keep your eyes open for God's good gifts to come to you along the way.

The Gift of Hope

IT'S A COMMON STORY. An addict or an alcoholic gets clean and sober and joins a life recovery group, and things start to look better. But then something triggers the old habits and behaviors—encountering a familiar point of pressure or spending time with an old friend from addiction days—and there's a relapse. Then the process of getting clean and sober starts all over again—beginning with a renewed sense of powerlessness.

It is essential that we stay the course in life recovery,

but doing so can also be discouraging or frustrating, especially at the beginning. As we admit—*again*—that our lives have become unmanageable, it's tempting to lose hope that things can ever be made right. But the apostle Paul tells us that we should actually "*glory* in our sufferings, because we know that suffering produces perseverance; perseverance, character; and character, hope. And hope does not put us to shame" (Romans 5:3-5, NIV, italics added). As we deal with the problems and trials in our lives, God gives us the gift of hope.

The road to recovery is like running a marathon. We don't wake up on the morning of a race and suddenly decide to enter and run. We would never finish the race that way. But there's a process that leads to success in running a long race. It's called *training*. There is also a type of training for dealing with our addictions, problems, and trials. It's called *life recovery*. And just as training for a race prepares us to run, life recovery sets us on a course to overcome our challenges and prepares us to receive the gift of hope.

Just as training for a race prepares us to run, life recovery prepares us to receive the gift of hope.

Roy has been in recovery for thirty-seven years. Recently, a friend asked him the age-old question: "Aren't you recovered by now? Why do you still go to Twelve Step meetings?"

Roy's first instinct was to say, *Well, it's called "recovery," not "the recovered."* Instead, he said, "I guess for me it has become a part of my life. It's not an ordeal, or something I wish I didn't have to do. The truth is, my friends are there, and they are my support system. God uses them in my recovery journey to give me hope, and I get to help others on their paths to recovery as well. When people who are just starting out see a guy who has been walking in recovery for thirty-seven years—well, that gives them hope that victory in their own lives is possible."

As he thought more about his answer, Roy added, "I don't struggle with the fear that I'm going to drink again. I guess you could say I've recovered from *that* issue. But there are so many other challenges in everyday life that I find I need the support and encouragement of my fellow strugglers, my recovery partners, to stay the course." Roy is both receiving and giving the gift of hope.

Millie's story is a little different. Though she has

been in recovery for twenty-one years, she hasn't been to a Twelve Step meeting in seven or eight years. For some people, that seems dangerous, as if she's asking for trouble. But Millie is quick to point out that she is still in recovery—she has only switched groups. Though she no longer goes to a Twelve Step meeting, she says that the group she now attends isn't much different from the Twelve Step groups she used to go to.

For more than a decade, she has been an active participant in a women's Bible study, where they not only study God's Word but also share what's going on in each other's lives.

Millie says, "It's just like my old recovery meetings, in that we are honest with each other, we don't hide our issues, and we are invested in each other's lives and families. That's where I get the encouragement and hope that keeps me on course."

She went on to explain that the women in her Bible study are divided into small groups of eight to ten, and that the same women have been in her small group for more than ten years now. They've all gotten to know each other very well, and they stay current in terms of life events and pressures.

"I get the same thing from my Bible study that I got from my recovery meetings," Millie says. "We are honest, accountable, and involved with each other throughout the week. They are my support system— and there's nothing we can't share within our small group." Millie is experiencing the gift of hope.

Both Roy and Millie discovered the gift of hope through the mystery of paradox—finding power in their powerlessness. They both started their recovery journeys years ago by recognizing

They discovered the gift of hope through the mystery of paradox—finding power in their powerlessness.

that they were powerless on their own to overcome their addictions. Prior to starting their recovery journey, they had tried a number of other ways to overcome their problems, always depending on their own power. Each time they failed, they eventually relapsed. They had hope, but they didn't know that the purpose of hope was to lead them to *training for endurance*. When they finally gave up striving on their own, they began to discover what it means to be powerless, which in turn allowed them to access real power—the power of God in their lives.

Though they didn't realize it at the time, they also discovered several biblical principles that pertain to training for endurance. For example, in Colossians 1:11, Paul prays that the Colossians would "be strengthened with all [God's] glorious power so you will have all the endurance and patience you need. May you be filled with joy." The strength for enduring the journey of recovery comes not from anything within ourselves but from the hope that comes from trusting in God's "glorious power," which he freely gives us when we ask.

The writer of the book of Hebrews encourages us to "strip off every weight that slows us down, especially the sin that so easily trips us up," and to "run with endurance the race God has set before us" (Hebrews 12:1). Building endurance is possible because of *faith*: "the confidence that what we hope for will actually happen" (Hebrews 11:1).

To experience the results of the gift of hope, we must get rid of the things that weigh us down—the difficult areas in our lives that we continually "try harder" to overcome. As the J. B. Phillips translation puts it, we're to rid ourselves of the sin that "dogs our feet." That's a great picture of the sin connected to our addictions—a dog that keeps nipping at our heels and tripping us up.

When we get involved in life recovery, we begin to identify things that truly weigh us down—the things we get anxious over and worry about—and we think about ways to get rid of them. We also become aware of how sin trips us up. What are the triggers that knock us off course? If we try to "just stop" our addictive issues without getting into recovery, we will miss both of these insights. The life recovery process sets us free from the weight of worry and the sins that cause us to stumble, so we can experience God's gift of hope to run the race successfully.

The Source of My Hope

Some people may say, "I can experience hope with just God at my side. Just God and me—we can do it! We don't need anyone else!" This attitude sounds noble, but it's a guaranteed way to miss the gift of hope. It is counterproductive to think that we can travel the life recovery journey on our own. That kind of thinking leads inevitably to failure and relapse. Both Roy and Millie tried that path, and both of them found that it didn't work. Now that they have seen the value of having support people in their lives, they would tell you that no one can persevere in recovery in isolation. They have succeeded in their recovery because they surrounded themselves with people who are available and supportive. God uses these people to give them hope.

Look at one of the traps we set for ourselves when we try to go it alone. When things start to get difficult—as they always do at some point—we typically pull back and withdraw from others as we struggle with our problems. Soon, the problems begin to grow, and we start feeling overwhelmed by our situation. Before we know it, we've relapsed. Now our hope is gone, and endurance is no longer the issue—getting back on track is. If we're isolated, we feel so much shame and guilt that even getting back on track seems to be a gigantic, insurmountable problem.

It is counterproductive to think that we can travel the life recovery journey on our own. That leads inevitably to failure and relapse.

Now look at the alternative. Things start to get difficult for us—again, as they always do at some point—but this time we are connected with our support system. We go to a meeting and listen as people share problems that are even bigger than ours—and yet they are staying on track. By sharing their struggles, they bring *hope* to the group. They aren't trying to do it alone, and we shouldn't either.

As we listen to these people describe their process, we begin to see our own problems from a different perspective. We still have our problems, but we draw courage and hope from listening to our friends describe what they are going through. Hearing how they are surviving inspires us to push forward and not give up. We also realize that, when we are the ones sharing our struggles, we are helping others to draw courage and hope from what we are going through.

Gradually—one day at a time, or even one moment at a time—we become aware that we are experiencing the gift of hope and it is leading us to a desirable outcome. It's a gift because it is beyond our ability to stay the course on our own. We become aware that not only are we able to overcome our addictions but also that others in our support system are encouraged to stay sober as well.

Hope always has an objective structure—the

means by which we have "confidence that what we hope for will actually happen." Structure "gives us assurance about things we cannot see" (Hebrews 11:1). But if we don't have structure, such as a Twelve Step program, our hope can become merely *wishful thinking*.

The apostle Paul reminds us that structure is needed for hope to become more than wishful thinking. He writes, "I pray that God, the source of hope, will fill you completely with joy and peace because you trust in him. Then you will overflow with confident hope through the power of the Holy Spirit" (Romans 15:13). Following God's plan of recovery, which the Bible calls *sanctification*, will cause our hope to overflow, bringing with it joy and peace.

The gift of hope is the motivation for our continuing on the same track when something is painful or difficult.

The dictionary defines *hope* as "desire accompanied by expectation of or belief in fulfillment."[1] Another definition is "believing that something good may happen." But this kind of hope—believing or expecting, but without the means of fulfillment—may lead us to disappointment. The gift of hope is the motivation for our continuing on the same track when something is painful or difficult. It's not simply the empty or casual sentiment of "I hope so." Its true meaning also involves our doing things that—through God's power—go beyond what we can do on our own. Its foundation is found in our relationship with God. That's why it is a gift. If we try to conjure up hope on our own, we will not be able to stay the course. We need our support people, and we need God's gift of hope to make it.

The Overflow of the Gift of Hope

As we discover the effects of the gift of hope, we not only experience transformation in the area of our addiction but also begin to see that the gift affects other areas of our lives as well. Roy talks about his struggle with alcohol, but he also talks about his issues with procrastination.

"Just like with my addiction," he said, "whenever something would go wrong, I found I would just give up. It didn't matter whether it was my sobriety, finishing a task at work, or some project that I had set for myself."

But when he got into recovery and gradually experienced the gift of hope, the triggers that would set him off and send him into relapse became less and less frequent.

"What surprised me, though," he said, "was that the more consistent I was in my recovery, the more I started to notice that I didn't give up like I used to when a problem reared its head in my work, or in some other project. I persisted until it was finished. That was new for me!"

Roy started to see that the gift of hope didn't apply only to his addiction; it gradually became a part of "the new Roy." But his hope was now founded on the reality of God and on God's gift to him. Others have said the same thing. As they stayed more consistently on track in their recovery (regardless of what they were recovering from), they also experienced the gift of hope in other areas of their lives. They experienced progress in all areas of life, not just where they had experienced problems.

The Misstep That Robs Us of Hope

The misstep that robs us of hope is characterized by this sort of thinking: "I can handle my problems just by trying harder, or by having more willpower." The truth about willpower is that its power is very limited. Anyone who has tried to diet knows only too well how limited our willpower really is. Anything based on will-power will work for a time; but eventually it will lose its power and we'll be right back where we started—struggling with feelings of hopelessness. That's why we need a power source that is greater that we are: We need God's intervention in our lives. Believing we can handle life on our own, just by trying harder or having more willpower, is the antithesis of hope.

The truth about willpower is that its power is very limited.

As our lives move forward, it's easy to forget what we used to experience. Under our own strength, we may have won some short-term victories, but no matter how hard we tried, we never experienced genuine hope based on our faith in God's power. According to a time-worn principle, "trying harder always gets you more of the same." That certainly was our experience before we started in recovery. No matter how hard we tried, nothing changed. The power source was missing.

Isaiah puts it this way: "Those who trust in the LORD will find new strength. They will soar high on wings like eagles. They will run and not grow weary. They will walk and not faint" (Isaiah 40:31). Under God's strength, we experience the transforming power that will give us the *hope* to carry us to the end. It is a gift that God wants to give us, and one that we desperately need to receive and experience.

Unwrapping the Gift of Hope

1. What tempts you to hold on to false hopes?

2. Describe a time when you had genuine hope and were disappointed. What contributed to your loss of hope?

3. How does *trying harder* undermine the gift of hope?

4. How does Step 1 of the Twelve Steps give you hope?

The Gift of Power

ONE OF THE BIG barriers for some of us who are contemplating recovery is having to start by declaring that we are powerless. *How can that change anything?* As a result, we often continue our fruitless search to find the power to change within ourselves. And each time we fail, we convince ourselves that if we had just tried a little harder, things would be different. It takes some people a long time to realize that doing *more* of whatever hasn't worked in the past isn't going to produce a different result.

Then there are those who realize that they don't have the power to change, but instead of taking responsibility for their actions, they say, "I don't know how that behavior happened again." They are like Sean, who is addicted to pornography. When he first started in recovery, he described his problem like this: "I don't know how, but it just happens. I'm doing something else, and all of a sudden I'm watching porn. I can go along for a period of time doing just fine—not even thinking about porn. Then, before I even realize it, I'm back watching it again and I don't know how I got there. It just happens. I think that's what they mean about being powerless. I certainly have no power, because I don't even realize I'm into it until I'm into it."

Sean was confused about the meaning of *powerlessness*. He thought that because his behavior seemed automatic to him, he was experiencing powerlessness. He didn't know where to go with his feelings; he just felt powerless. He needed to see that his behavior wasn't in fact automatic; at some point, he was making a choice. Once he was able to see and recognize the decisions he was making, he began to understand the true nature of his powerlessness.

Admitting that we are powerless over our problems in Step 1 of the Twelve Steps doesn't mean we don't have a choice in the matter. In order to act out, we first must decide to act out. We may not always be aware that we're making a decision, but it's never just automatic.

Admitting that we are powerless over our problems doesn't mean we don't have a choice in the matter.

For some time, Sean fought the idea that he was making a decision at some point in the process of his actions. He needed to understand that being powerless didn't mean he couldn't help acting out; it meant that he was powerless *on his own* to make the right choices. It wasn't until he saw that his behavior resulted from his unwillingness to take responsibility that he began to understand the concept of powerlessness in the recovery process. He thought that, if his behavior was automatic (which he mistakenly thought it was), then he couldn't help it, and that therefore he wasn't responsible.

He finally came to realize that, even though he was unable to make the right choices in his own strength, he still had a choice. It wasn't automatic.

He had to recognize that when he said, "I can't," what he really meant was "I won't." And the *I won't* was founded on his failure to take responsibility for his actions.

When he finally acknowledged that his acting out didn't "just happen," he started to identify the triggers that led him to make the wrong choices. He was able to see that he had developed patterns of behavior that were stronger than he was.

In the previous chapter, we talked about the paradox of powerlessness. To recognize our powerlessness is always an *I can't*. We *recognize* the problem; we *own* the problem; we even *confess* the problem; and then we turn to God for help. This turns *I can't* into *God can!* But a failure to recognize, own, and confess our problems leaves us stuck and eventually leads to an attitude of *I won't*.

> We must recognize that we are unable to overcome our problem behaviors on our own—we need the gift of God's power.

Choosing powerlessness starts with taking responsibility for our problem behaviors. Its purpose is to put an end to our weak efforts to improve on our own. We must recognize that we are unable to overcome our problem behaviors on our own—we need the gift of God's power. How do we know when we have received the gift of power? Things begin changing for the better in our lives!

The Promise of the Gift of Power

God wants to empower us to do things we cannot do on our own. As the apostle Paul said to his young protégé Timothy, "God has not given us a spirit of fear and timidity, but of power, love, and self-discipline" (2 Timothy 1:7). Paul extends this theme when he tells the Corinthians, "We now have this light shining in our hearts, but we ourselves are like fragile clay jars containing this great treasure. This makes it clear that our great power is from God, not from ourselves" (2 Corinthians 4:7). God gifts us with his power.

When we begin our recovery, we certainly feel like fragile clay jars. We know we're on the right path, but at the beginning we feel as if we're going to be smashed to pieces by our problems. Admitting that we are powerless leads us to turn to God and receive the gift of his "great power." We will never find it within ourselves—it is a gift from God!

Paul knew that he didn't have enough power within himself to be transformed. But he knew the source of that power: "I want to know Christ and experience the mighty power that raised him from the dead" (Philippians 3:10). The more we know Christ, the more we experience God's power. What an awesome promise! God's gift of power to us is the same power he used in resurrecting Christ from the dead.

When we followed Step 3 of the Twelve Steps and "made a decision to turn our wills and our lives over to the care of God," we prayed. As a result, we were given God's power. In our recovery, we followed the injunction in James 5:16 to "confess your sins to each other and pray for each other so that you may be healed. The earnest prayer of a righteous person has great power and produces wonderful results." Through prayer we gain access to the gift of power. We find that God loves to give us his gifts, and he wants to give us his power.

The more we know Christ, the more we experience God's power. What an awesome promise!

Peter sums up God's promise of the gift of power when he writes, "By his divine power, God has given us everything we need for living a godly life" (2 Peter 1:3). We are empowered by God's divine power. It comes from God, not from somewhere deep inside us. As we cease striving and begin to acknowledge in prayer the gift of God's power in our lives, we experience growth in our recovery.

The Evidence of God's Gift of Power

Have you thought about how incredible it is to stand up in front of a group of strangers and share something that has been your secret for years or even decades? For as long as we have struggled with our addictions, we have done so in secret. Secrecy was the watchword—*no one must know*. And now we dare to share the secret, not just with a trusted friend but with a group of people we are just getting to know. That goes so far beyond the fear and insecurity that drove our addiction that we can hardly believe it is us doing the sharing.

Now, instead of hiding from people out of our fear of being known, we are making a fearless moral inventory of ourselves and sharing it with another person. That takes a power that can come only from outside ourselves. That takes divine power. We are now willing to be known by others—and even more important, to be known by ourselves.

For those of us who are naturally outgoing, we have always made certain that our friendliness never reached very far beneath the surface. Others may have known a few things about us, but no one knew who we really were. For those whose personality is more reserved, it probably has been easy to stay on the surface. Regardless of our personal style, we made certain we were not found out! But now we are committed to a sponsor and to our group, and a major part of that commitment is to be known at deeper levels.

Now that we have God's power at work in us, we are stronger. Our relapses are less frequent or are nonexistent.

Earlier, when we slipped and fell, we felt like giving up. In fact, many times we did just that—we gave up and wallowed for a time in our misery. But now that we have God's power at work in us, we are stronger. Our relapses are less frequent or are nonexistent. When we relapse, we quickly get up, call a friend, and figure out what triggered our failure. We don't waste any time before we get right back on the path of our recovery. We now have the gift of God's power and that makes a huge difference.

Sean has found that his relapses aren't "automatic" anymore. As he took responsibility for his failures rather than explaining to himself and others that they "just happened," he saw that he was still making bad choices. But he was also experiencing more and more of God's power in his life as he openly shared his story with others, including some whom he had previously determined would never know about his problem.

He also put together an accountability group and included some men who he knew would be tough on him. He had actually been afraid of one of the three men to whom he is now accountable, and for that reason he never would have chosen him. But with God's gift of power in Sean's life, he is now determined to succeed. He knows that facing this man's toughness is a measure of how serious he is about his own recovery. Sean recognizes that there is a major difference in his life, and he is determined that, with

God's help, each day will now be an expression of that difference.

The Misstep That Robs Us of God's Power

No one plans to relapse. Relapse is much more subtle than that. For example, an alcoholic has been sober for months, and he is really working the program. He feels much stronger—too strong, in fact—and so he thinks he will stop by the bar and visit with some of his old drinking buddies. He fully intends to have only sparkling water . . .

Or take the sex addict who is doing so well in recovery that he forgets his triggers. He then relaxes, watches something on TV he knows he shouldn't watch, and suddenly has a relapse.

Or take the prescription-drug addict who is doing well in her recovery but gets tired of going to meetings. She decides to stay home. It doesn't take very long for her to get bored, and the next day she is back in a doctor's office asking for a refill.

The misstep that robs us of God's power is often articulated this way: "After making good progress in my recovery, I can start using again in moderation."

What each of these people didn't realize was

something that a recovering alcoholic named Joe once described in a meeting: We don't have the power on our own to resist. We must rely on the power of God to make the right choices.

Joe had been in Mexico, at a place where the margaritas were flowing in a fountain, free for anyone with a glass to enjoy. He knew he had to leave, and he did. He later said, "I think that when I die and they put me in my coffin, my addiction will be there right next to me. And before they close the lid, my addiction will sit up and say, 'Come on, Joe, let's just have one more for the road!'" He knew that within himself, he did not have to power to stay the course. And he wasn't going to jeopardize his on-going recovery by sitting in a place full of temptation.

We don't have the power on our own to resist. We must rely on the power of God to make the right choices.

In each of these cases, no one was planning to relapse. They just started to feel too good about their progress in recovery. They forgot the adage of "one day at a time." They thought that the gift of power was now somehow based on how well they were doing. They forgot that the power they were experiencing was God's power, which was given to them as a gift. That gift needed to be protected.

When we are on a solid path of recovery, the last thing we want to do is think we can now control what has been controlling us. "As a dog returns to its vomit, so a fool repeats his foolishness" (Proverbs 26:11). This proverb is a vivid picture of what we do when we think we are strong enough within ourselves to go back to our old haunts without falling back into our old behaviors.

Paul warns us, "If you think you are standing strong, be careful not to fall" (1 Corinthians 10:12).

> *Nothing will defeat our progress faster than the attitude that says, "Now I think I can do it on my own."*

Some people who have been in recovery for many years return tragically, and even fatally, to their old behaviors when something goes wrong in their lives. People who don't understand the power of addiction cannot understand why that would happen. But when we are in recovery, we come to realize the power of our old behaviors. Never, ever think that the gift of power has transferred to you and that you now own it within yourself. We don't have the power to stay the course within ourselves alone. Nothing will defeat our progress faster than the attitude that says, "Now I think I can do it on my own."

Unwrapping the Gift of Power

1. How would you describe *power* as being a gift?

2. When you accepted your powerlessness, how did it empower you?

3. How does *relapse* relate to the gift of power?

4. How has the gift of power affected other areas of your life?

The Gift of Character

WHEN PEOPLE LOSE their character, they often don't realize the depth of their loss. One of the costs of addiction is that we lose our integrity and are seen as having questionable character. We no longer act well in our dealings with people, truthfulness seems to become optional, our sense of morality is weakened, and we are characterized by others as no longer being trustworthy. It doesn't take much to destroy good character, and character takes a long time to repair.

Integrity is a major ingredient of good character.

King David believed that maintaining his integrity was central to who he was as a man of God: "May integrity and honesty protect me, for I put my hope in you" (Psalm 25:21). In another psalm, he writes, "Don't let me suffer the fate of sinners. . . . I am not like that; I live with integrity. So redeem me and show me mercy" (Psalm 26:9, 11). Psalm 119:1 says, "Joyful are people of integrity, who follow the instructions of the LORD."

When Larry was using drugs, he would not have characterized himself as joyful or a person of integrity. He was skillful at never telling the truth, and he was a thief—if he wanted something of yours that wasn't bolted down, it would be gone. His friends wouldn't stick around because they felt that Larry used them for his own purposes. After all, that's what a drug addiction does to a person. Being a man of good character was the furthest thing from Larry's mind—he was concerned only about his next fix.

He hadn't started out that way. Before becoming curious about how certain prescription drugs could change his mood, he was basically an honest young man. But his curiosity led to experimentation, his experimentation led to addiction, and his addiction progressed beyond prescription meds to include illegal drugs. Larry ended up living on the street. He began doing whatever he needed to do to survive, and that included feeding his addiction. It wasn't until his only friend died from an overdose that Larry finally faced reality and sought help. He has been clean and sober now for more than ten years.

Today, when he tells his story in a meeting or shares some part of his story with a friend, the life he now lives stands in stark contrast to the life he once had. He has received, and continues to receive, the gift of character. Today, he is considered a trustworthy member of his community.

One way to define good character is by the level of a person's trustworthiness, which includes honesty and reliability.

"I surely did not possess that trait when I was using," Larry says, "but God has gifted me with healing and has given me a renewed character. Others know me now as honest, and they know they can trust me."

Other characteristics of good character include the ability to show respect and become worthy of the respect of others. In his recovery, Larry has learned to take responsibility for what happens in his life. He has a sense of fairness in his relationships and truly cares about other people.

Building respect and becoming responsible are not always easy. The gift of character comes in bits and pieces as we faithfully work through Steps 4–7. These are painful Steps, as we look deep within ourselves at the consequences of our lack of integrity and actually admit to someone else our failures and character defects. But we must experience this process of brokenness because it lays the foundation for receiving the gift of good character. That's what it means to be "entirely ready for God to remove all these defects of character."

One way to define good character is by the level of a person's trustworthiness, which includes honesty and reliability.

Larry found that he had to give up his need to control everything in his life—a skill that had kept him alive when he was on the streets. But tackling Step 7 goes beyond willingness and readiness; it involves "asking God to remove our shortcomings."

Larry found that when he asked God to do that, God's way of giving the gift of good character wasn't the way that Larry would have chosen. He had to learn the same lesson that the prophet Jeremiah learned when God told him to "go down to the potter's shop" in Jeremiah 18:2. Jeremiah did as he was told "and found the potter working at his wheel. But the jar he was making did not turn out as he had hoped, so he crushed it into a lump of clay and started over. Then the LORD gave me this message: '. . . Can I not do to you as this potter has done to his clay? As the clay is in the potter's hand, so are you in my hand'" (Jeremiah 18:3-6). God's ways are not our ways. We think that good character can be taught, but character is a gift that God gives us as we humbly ask for his help.

We think that good character can be taught, but character is a gift that God gives us as we humbly ask for his help.

As Larry worked Steps 4 through 7, he found that God was faithful to hear his prayer and answer it. Larry gets affirmation from his family and friends that he has changed. "The old Larry is back," they say, and they all rejoice. He hasn't fully arrived, but he is on the right path.

Larry uses a favorite passage from Paul's letter to

the Galatians to measure how his gift of character is developing: "The Holy Spirit produces this kind of fruit in our lives: love, joy, peace, patience, kindness, goodness, faithfulness, gentleness, and self-control. There is no law against these things! Those who belong to Christ Jesus have nailed the passions and desires of their sinful nature to his cross and crucified them there" (Galatians 5:22-24). When Larry talks about this passage, he adds, "God is still working on the patience part of the gift, as well as one or two other aspects."

Qualities of good character are the fruit of the Spirit. Instead of being self-absorbed in our addictions, we learn to love others and to express kindness and gentleness in our relationships. Instead of the anxiety of struggling just to maintain the status quo of our destructive behavior, we begin to experience peace and joy in our lives. Our desperate drive to control life's situations changes to the expression of self-control. And patience and faithfulness replace the pattern of using people for our own ends. These traits are clear evidence that God is at work in his own way, helping us to experience his gift of character in our lives.

What Is Character?

The dictionary defines *character* as "the moral and mental qualities distinctive to an individual."[1] This definition includes the idea that character is an expression of our reputation. Abraham Lincoln once said, "Perhaps a man's character was like a tree and his reputation like its shadow. The shadow is what we think of it; the tree is the real thing."[2] To use Lincoln's analogy, the tree can be either good or bad. When we say that a person "has no character," that isn't good. The apostle Paul tells us that "bad company corrupts good character" (1 Corinthians 15:33). When we live in our addictions, we don't hang around people of character. We're more comfortable with "bad company." Consequently, we corrupt our own virtue.

A person with poor character can be described as someone who seeks instant gratification, makes a practice of telling lies and stealing from others, uses other people, and lives in the shady places where corruption thrives. Obviously, the absence of good character is one of the consequences of an addiction. One who simply stops an addictive behavior isn't prepared to receive the gift of good character. That's really what recovery is all about—laying the groundwork for receiving this gift.

When we are active in our addictions, life doesn't run smoothly. When we begin our recovery, life still doesn't run smoothly. But Paul tells us what to do during the early stages of our recovery: *rejoice.* "We can rejoice, too, when we run into problems and trials, for we know that they help us develop endurance. And endurance develops strength of character, and character strengthens our confident hope of salvation" (Romans 5:3-4). As we seek to develop our new life in Christ and to win the battle against our addictions, we will experience problems and trials, many of which are the consequences of our former behavior. But Paul says we should rejoice when these things happen, for there are two guaranteed results—one is the gift of endurance, which we've already looked at; the other is the gift of character. When we experience the gift of good character, it will lead us to a confident hope.

> *When we live in our addictions, we don't hang around people of character. We're more comfortable with "bad company."*

The Evidence of the Gift of Character

Working the Twelve Steps in our recovery prepares the groundwork for the gift of character. In fact, Steps 4 through 7 could be called the character-building Steps, for they open us to developing integrity and virtue. Look at the process: We begin with Step 4, when we take a fearless moral inventory of ourselves. We begin to look at our own shortcomings rather than blaming others for them. We begin to consider where we have fallen short in terms of the "four absolutes": honesty, purity, unselfishness, and love.

That process alone is hard enough, but then Step 5 tells us to share our inventory with God—making it a matter of prayer—and to share it with someone we trust. Step 6 reminds us that we must be ready for God to remove our negative character traits, and Step 7 directs us to humbly ask God to remove them from us. As we faithfully work through these four crucial steps, we are preparing the soil of our lives, into which God implants the gift of character. Once we've completed our moral inventory—cataloguing our loss of character—we can ask God to remove these negative characteristics and replace them with the four positive traits of honesty, purity, unselfishness, and love.

The Misstep That Robs Us of the Gift of Character

By this point in your recovery, you may have heard about people called *one-steppers*, who believe that only one step is necessary—turning their lives over to Jesus Christ. Repenting of our sins and turning our wills and lives over to the care of God is one of the Twelve Steps; to one-steppers, it's the only step. But turning our lives over to Christ is just the beginning. It doesn't instantly establish and build our character or make us mature in our faith. We call working through the Twelve Steps *life recovery*, but the Bible uses the word *sanctification* for the same process.

Turning our lives over to Christ is just the beginning. It doesn't instantly establish and build our character or make us mature in our faith.

The writer to the Hebrews says,

> Solid food is for those who are mature, who through training have the skill to recognize the difference between right and wrong. So let

us stop going over the basic teachings about Christ again and again. Let us go on instead and become mature in our understanding. Surely we don't need to start again with the fundamental importance of repenting from evil deeds and placing our faith in God.

HEBREWS 5:14–6:1

It seems as if the writer is addressing those who, like the one-steppers, believe that walking with Jesus is as simple as turning their lives over to him—and the rest "just happens." They might as well say, "Forget about maturing in the faith; forget about the need for life recovery!"

Our walk of faith is similar to the process of life recovery. We begin with a decision and then follow that decision with a process that brings healing, wholeness, and growth. It's the *process* that produces the fruit of the Spirit. But it's not automatic. We must continue to move forward in growth and maturity. Gradually we heal, and gradually we receive the gift of character.

Often when we were trying in our own strength to break free from our addictions, we would plead with God to "fix us." Then we followed that plea with the word *now*! The problem is compounded by our knowledge that God sometimes does fix things quickly. Sometimes the cravings, the addictive parts, are removed quickly. But when that occurs, it is a gift that marks the *beginning* of recovery, which is a healing, sanctifying, and maturing process. However God acts—quickly or slowly—his actions have a purpose. We need to accept it and move forward. Either way, it is not by our own strength or power that we grow and mature; it is by the power of the Holy Spirit.

Unwrapping the Gift of Character

1. What does it mean to say that someone has *good character*?

2. How do Steps 4–7 help us develop our character?

3. How can "one-stepping" cause us to miss the gift of character?

4. How are *recovery* and *sanctification* similar? How do they differ?

4

The Gift of Clarity

DENIAL IS A MECHANISM that accompanies every addiction. Typically, we think that a person is in denial in order to fool other people. But the mechanism of denial is actually designed to fool ourselves. Our thinking is distorted. No matter how much we are confronted by reality, the fog of denial is at work, and the mantra is, "I don't have a problem. I don't know what you're so worried about." We've all expressed sentiments similar to that, but usually not to fool the other person about our problem; we just want to get him or her off our back.

Jenny had more than just a problem. Her addiction had created a crisis. But according to her, she had almost everything under control—just a few loose ends here and there. The truth was that she was addicted to gambling, which is called a process addiction (as opposed to a chemical addiction). Regardless of the extent of the financial crisis she had created, she would emphatically deny that there was a problem.

"I just need a few more winning streaks and everything will be okay," she would say.

Reality existed somewhere outside of her mental fog.

Jenny's addiction started out innocently on the Internet. When her husband, Ed, had to work evenings, she became bored. She had seen an ad on TV about a website where people could gamble on the Internet. And of course they had made it look like fun. So she checked it out, registered, and started playing. Sometimes she even won some money. *Wow*, she thought, *it's like free money*.

Eventually, she got bored with Internet gambling and wondered whether there was a casino nearby. Sure enough, when she checked, she found one about twenty miles from her home. One evening, she left a note for Ed and drove to the casino. She had about a hundred dollars in her purse, and she vowed that she would leave when the money ran out. It took a while—the machines were generous that evening, and it wasn't until about five o'clock in the morning that her hundred dollars were gone. She had spent the evening playing the slot machines, but she decided to watch the poker tables for a while. About an hour later, she headed home.

Her husband wasn't happy about her being gone all night. He was worried about her driving that far alone, especially at night. But Jenny talked about how much fun she'd had, and that quieted Ed's concerns. She did have fun and was ready to do it again, but she needed some time to gather enough cash to play again. And the next time, she spent a big part of the evening watching the poker tables.

Eventually, she rationalized both to her husband and to herself her enjoyment of her casino visits by noting that she didn't go very often and that she was careful not to add to her losses with the ATM machine. Ed tried to understand, telling himself that it was good for her to have a break in her routine.

Over time, the problem grew. Sometimes she'd sneak off to the casino during the day, thinking Ed wouldn't notice. Gradually her $100 limit grew to $300. She was still determined not to use the ATM, but sometimes it sure looked tempting—especially when she thought she was on the verge of a winning streak. There were several times, after she had started waking up around two o'clock in the morning thinking about the casino, when she decided to quit trying to get back to sleep and just got up to head out to the casino.

It wasn't long before she and Ed began fighting about her "too frequent" visits to the casino. Jenny learned to lie about her losses, focusing instead on the times when she won and came out ahead. At some level, she wondered whether she was acting a little compulsively, but the chance that she might win big kept her from really examining how addicted she had become. Besides, it wasn't alcohol or drugs; it was just having some fun at the casino. As always, addiction thrives on denial.

Addiction thrives on denial.

It wasn't until her husband found out that bills weren't being paid because there was no money that he finally accepted the fact that Jenny had a problem. He talked with some friends, who suggested that he start going to meetings. That was where he learned that Jenny's problem was also his problem. Because of the financial crisis they were now facing, he convinced Jenny to start going to a Twelve Step meeting as well.

It took almost three years of hard work for Jenny and Ed to untangle the knots that Jenny had created in their finances. During those three years, both Ed and Jenny came to understand how gambling can really be an addiction. They realized that they had been seduced by their own *stinkin' thinkin'*. Neither one was looking at reality. They were in a fog. As they grew in their recovery, they started to see things realistically. Jenny realized not only that she had denied to Ed that she had a problem, but also that her denial kept her from seeing her own problem. Some of her distorted thinking included the following rationalizations:

"As long as I don't use the ATM, I don't have a problem."

"I'm not really that far behind in my winnings."

"How can something that's so fun be a
    problem?"
"What Ed doesn't know won't hurt him."
"Maybe this time I'll win enough to catch up
    financially."

Ed's distorted thinking included the following excuses:

"She's just having fun."
"As long as I make enough money, it can't be
    a problem."
"I trust Jenny—she's so responsible with our
    money."
"Everything would be fine if only she would
    answer her phone."
"She's the one with the problem."

The Need for the Gift of Clarity

When our thinking becomes distorted, confusion
reigns. Confusion is the most common state of
mind among people actively involved in an addiction. They are confused about who they are, where
they are headed, and even what they are looking for
in doing what they are doing. Reality begins to fade

into the background, then fades completely away. Attempts to resolve the daily problems only lead to additional problems because of the confusion. It's like what Paul describes in 1 Corinthians 13:12: "Now we see things imperfectly, like puzzling reflections in a mirror, but then we will see everything with perfect clarity." To an addict of any kind, the world looks like a puzzling reflection in a mirror. Eventually, we get to the point where we don't even try to make sense of it.

It's clear that Paul is speaking here about what happens when we move from life on earth to life in heaven—then we will see all things clearly. But this Scripture passage also describes what happens when our thinking gets distorted. When we are actively in recovery, we receive the gift of seeing things with clarity, and the truth comes back into focus. We especially begin to see ourselves with clarity. There is a quality of coherence and intelligibility in how we interpret what we observe. The gift of clarity could be defined as the absence of denial—even the absence of a *need* for denial. Instead,

> *When we are actively in recovery, we receive the gift of seeing things with clarity, and the truth comes back into focus.*

there is transparency, even purity, in how we present ourselves and see ourselves.

When we receive the gift of clarity, we become more in touch with reality. We can look at situations, our condition, and our behavior and see what is needed to meet our challenges. We are more likely to make wise choices about our future and to know what needs to be done about the present. We also can see a way to do what needs to be done. There is an honesty in how we describe reality. No cover-up is needed when we have the gift of clarity.

The Misstep That Robs Us of the Gift of Clarity

Both Jenny and Ed avoided the crucial misstep that can cancel out the gift of clarity—that is, the belief that, because we are accountable to God, we don't need a sponsor or anyone else to help us in our recovery. Jenny and Ed didn't try to solve their problem on their own. Something about having a sponsor says to others—and especially to ourselves—that we are serious about our recovery and about breaking the cycle of our addiction.

We still are accountable to God, but God has designed his relationship with us to be experienced through community. How can we relate to a God whom we cannot see unless we can relate to other people whom we can? God often chooses to work in our lives through other people: "As iron sharpens iron, so a friend sharpens a friend" (Proverbs 27:17). The "sharpening" that a friend or a sponsor provides for us is part of the gift of clarity.

The problem of confusion is compounded by the fact that, whenever we look at ourselves, we do so from a subjective stance. It is very difficult to be objective about ourselves. That's part of the reason why we need the help of others if we are to understand ourselves. As we've seen, denial is a process that primarily shields us from the truth about ourselves. It also is an attempt to keep others from knowing the truth about us, even though at some level we suspect they can see through our denial. But we can't see ourselves as we really are without the help of a sponsor and a group of friends.

It is very difficult to be objective about ourselves. That's part of the reason why we need the help of others if we are to understand ourselves.

When we mistakenly think that recovery is something that takes place between ourselves and God alone, we miss the point. We are accountable to God, yes, but we will grow so much stronger when we have a sponsor to guide us, encourage us, and hold us accountable. Our sponsor is the point person in that process. He or she isn't perfect any more than we are. But a sponsor has been on the journey of recovery and knows some of the pitfalls and challenges we will face in our own recovery. Sponsors are human guides who keep us accountable to themselves and to God.

Unwrapping the Gift of Clarity

1. When you were actively struggling with your addiction or problem, how did *denial* keep you from the gift of clarity?

2. Give some examples of how your thinking was distorted when you were active in your addiction.

3. How would you define the benefits of the gift of clarity?

4. How have others helped you experience the gift of clarity?

5

The Gift of Security

IT'S AMAZING, the risks an addict will take to maintain an addiction. One man recounted how he had confronted his drug dealer because he thought the dealer wasn't playing fair—and he ended up with a permanent scar on his lip. As this man reflects on it today, he realizes he was lucky to get only a split lip. Others he has known encountered far more serious consequences.

Talk to anyone in recovery, and they can tell you stories about close calls they had while actively living in their addiction. Sam told about the time he was desperate for his next fix. He had been studying what appeared to be an abandoned car down the street from where he had been staying for several weeks. He thought it was at least worth a try to steal it, so he called a junkyard that would pay cash for undrivable cars and pick them up. It was easy, he thought, until he was arrested for stealing the car. Apparently, it wasn't abandoned after all, and when the owner reported it stolen, it didn't take long to trace the theft back to Sam. He spent almost a year in jail for that little episode.

Some years later, he was surprised to learn that he could have been charged with a felony, but somehow the low value of the car turned a felony into a misdemeanor. Once he got into recovery, he checked back on his record to see how it would affect a job search. He was surprised when he realized that all of his arrests had been misdemeanors—there were no felonies on his record. "It was like someone had been protecting me from myself," he said.

Laura and her roommate, Jessica, were both so far under the influence of the drugs they were taking that they couldn't control their thoughts, and they obsessed about committing suicide. They talked about it all the time. Eventually, they started to plan how they would do it. Then Laura did something that got her arrested. While in jail waiting for her trial, she received word that Jessica had tied together several bed sheets and had committed suicide by hanging herself outside their second-story window. That had been their plan! But Laura was in jail and was coming off her drug-induced suicidal thoughts. She was horrified at what Jessica had done but even more horrified at the realization that, before she was arrested, she had been preparing to do the same thing.

When we experience God's protection in our recovery, it is his gift to us—the gift of security.

After Laura recounted her story at a recent meeting, a young woman came up to her and shared her own story, which was very similar to Laura's. Then the woman added, "For some reason, it took something bad to happen—for me to be arrested and to spend the next two years in prison—just to protect me from myself."

Why did Sam, Laura, and the other young woman experience what seemed to be God's protection while active in their addictions? We don't know.

God's ways are not our ways, and we will never fully understand. All we can do is thank him. When we experience God's protection in our recovery, it is his gift to us—the gift of security.

The Gift of Security Defined

When we look up the definition of *security*, it applies to both situations we've just described. It can be defined as "the state of being free from danger or threat."[1] It also involves the idea of feeling safe, stable, and free from fear or anxiety. Somehow, both Sam and Laura were protected from themselves before beginning their recovery. But they will now experience the freedom from danger or threat that comes with recovery—the gift of security.

It is a gift that we receive and can count on when we are seriously engaged with our recovery. Look at what the apostle Paul tells us: "The law of Moses was unable to save us because of the weakness of our sinful nature. So God did what the law could not do. He sent his own Son in a body like the bodies we sinners have. And in that body God declared an end to sin's control over us by giving his Son as a sacrifice for our sins" (Romans 8:3). How amazing. We can be secure in our salvation because it is a gift from God. The gift of security is received through our growing faith, and its power is the power of God himself.

Obviously, having the gift of security doesn't mean we won't experience trials and temptations. In several places in the Bible, we are told to rejoice when we face life's trials—they are part of life. When we realize that we are secure in our relationship with God, our response to these problems is that we can rejoice. The purpose of trials is to teach us things, to keep us focused on our recovery, and to help us grow stronger in our faith.

The purpose of trials is to teach us things, to keep us focused on our recovery, and to help us grow stronger in our faith.

Though we are secure in Christ, we aren't protected from life itself. To be alive is to encounter trials and problems at times. Our security is rooted in the fact that God is on our side. Paul reminds us that "God is faithful. He will not allow the temptation to be more than you can stand. When you are tempted, he will show you a way out so that you can endure" (1 Corinthians 10:13). The gift of security is God's provision to protect us as we lean on his strength.

As we are faithful and stand in awe of God and his power, we can feel secure in our relationship with God. He will provide a way for us. That's God's gift to those of us who are faithful to our recovery path. But it requires not only the attitude of faith, it also requires patience. God's timetable is not our timetable. He often acts more slowly than we would like. Patience teaches us to develop trust in God. As we trust in God, we will begin to experience and understand his purpose in our lives.

Having an attitude of faith, being patient, and trusting that God has a purpose—each of these cannot be done in isolation. That's why we need to be connected to other people on the same path of growth and recovery. We share our struggles in order to encourage others and be encouraged by others. When we are open to our fellow travelers on the journey to life recovery, we will find that we are open to what God wants to do in our lives.

Secure from What?

Now the question is, *Why do we need to feel secure?* All it takes to answer that question is to think back to what life was like before we started in recovery.

When we were out there on our own, in the midst of our addictions, we often fell into relational traps that ended up hurting us terribly. The company we kept was bad company—after all, we didn't hang around people who were doing the right things with their lives, because that would have been too threatening for us. No, we spent our time with people who were living in the shadows just as we were. There was no security in any of that.

Now that we are in recovery, it's hard to believe we actually spent time with, and listened to, those people. But that was part of where we were. Obviously, we weren't going to talk to or listen to someone who was winning at life. That would have called into question everything we were doing wrong.

We also had wrong attitudes, and we still need to be protected from lapsing back into those ways of thinking. For example, when we were active in our addictions, we believed that all of our problems were the fault of other people. And because we couldn't change other people, we felt that our situation was hopeless. We also nursed the idea that everyone and everything was lined up against us. How could we beat the system when everything was stacked against

When we were active in our addictions, we believed that all of our problems were the fault of other people.

us? Taking responsibility for our behavior, for our situations, and for our assumed hopelessness was the furthest thing from our minds.

If, during that time, we had run across Romans 8:31—"If God is for us, who can ever be against us?"—we probably would have concluded that God wasn't for us, that he was one of those who were against us. But if we had continued reading, we would have gotten the full story:

> Since he did not spare even his own Son but gave him up for us all, won't he also give us everything else? Who dares accuse us whom God has chosen for his own? No one—for God himself has given us right standing with himself. Who then will condemn us? No one—for Christ Jesus died for us and was raised to life for us, and he is sitting in the place of honor at God's right hand, pleading for us.
>
> ROMANS 8:32-34

With a God who loves us like that—who gave everything for us—we have the foundation for believing he wants to give us his gift of security.

The Misstep That Robs Us of the Gift of Security

Sometimes, we opt out of the healing process of recovery. When we short-circuit the process of recovery, we will also miss out on the gift of security. Those at risk of losing the gift of security often say things that sound something like this: "Well, recovery might be good for some people, but it just isn't right for me." Then they might add, "I'm doing it my way, and so far it's working for me." Or they might say, "I tried recovery, but it wasn't really that helpful. I think I can do it better by myself—I think I know what I need."

The problem with this attitude is something Paul warns us about. He writes, "You must continue to believe this truth and stand firmly in it. Don't drift away from the assurance you received when you heard the Good News" (Colossians 1:23). When we made the decision to surrender ourselves to God, we believed the truth that our lives were out of control. We accepted that truth and surrendered our lives to

Jesus Christ. That was a very bold move, and it set us on the course of healing and recovery.

But often we try to do the next Steps in the healing process *our* way, which usually involves doing it alone. We think, *If I'm going to do Step 4, why do I have to do Step 5?* So we don't take Step 4 seriously, and our enemy becomes what Paul calls a tendency to *drift*—to move away from the place of surrender and thus start to compromise, and even jeopardize, the great progress we have made. We ease up a little here, and then a little there, and soon we have forgotten the power we experienced when we surrendered our lives to God.

When we made the decision to surrender ourselves to God, we believed the truth that our lives were out of control.

We may gradually drift away from going to meetings. We don't intentionally stop going; we simply neglect the need to attend. We forget the progress we made when we went to thirty meetings in thirty days—how it strengthened our resolve to stay the course. Maybe we still try to get to a meeting once a week, but at the same time we're drifting away from our recovery and losing the path of growth and maturity.

Don't get caught up in drifting! Stay the course. Stay involved. Work with a sponsor, and do the program the way it has worked for countless other people. Make perseverance your response to the gift of security!

Unwrapping the Gift of Security

1. Give some examples of how God has protected you during your recovery.

2. Rewrite Romans 8:31-38, personalizing it with your name.

3. From whom do you currently seek advice? How has that helped you to experience the gift of security?

4. How has having a good sponsor increased your sense of security? Be specific.

6

The Gift of Abundance

WHEN WE ARE LIVING out our addictions, we eventually come to the place where almost all of our resources are aimed toward feeding the addiction. As for the other aspects of our lives, we get used to the idea of barely getting by. But sometimes the attitude that we don't have enough precedes the addiction. It may even be a factor in the development of some addictions, especially when the addiction is related to food.

We panic at the thought of running out of

whatever we're addicted to. We stash away alcohol in different places so there is always some available. We're careful to make sure that we always have some of our drug of choice on hand. Even with gambling, we live in fear that the money will run out. When it comes to food addictions, the fear is that we will run out of our comfort food, our source of soothing.

For Sarah, using food as a source of comfort began during her childhood, and well into her adult years she felt that it was essential to always have something sweet to eat in the privacy of her room.

Sarah had been molested by her uncle, her mother's brother, when she was six years old. When she tried to tell her mother what had happened, her mother didn't believe her. In fact, from that time forward, it seemed that her mother was always angry with her, that all her negative emotions became focused on Sarah.

The truth was Sarah's mother couldn't face the fact that her brother had done the same thing to her when she was a young girl. Perhaps her shame at not protecting Sarah, coupled with her own hurt and anger at what her brother had done to her, led her not to believe Sarah.

Of course, Sarah didn't know anything about this at the time. The angrier her mother became with her, the more Sarah retreated into herself, spending more and more time alone in her room. And when she was alone, it felt nice to eat something sweet for comfort.

When her mother went food shopping, Sarah often helped her unpack the groceries. It was easy to take a bag of cookies and sneak them into her room. Or she would simply take a half bag of chips from the pantry and store it in her room. Eventually, she had a miniature grocery store hidden away. It felt to Sarah as if she could never get enough to eat. She didn't like eating with her mother, and having a stash of cookies, chips, and other snacks helped her not to feel her pain. It also helped her deal with her isolation within the family.

She had an irrational scarcity mind-set that wasn't based on the reality of the situation. But it was her reality.

By the time Sarah started high school, she wasn't obese, but she was definitely overweight. When the stock in her mini-grocery grew thin, she developed a fear that she "wouldn't have enough" to eat. Even though it wasn't true in the real sense, she would panic whenever she thought about it. She had an irrational scarcity mind-set that wasn't based on the reality of the situation. But it was *her* reality, and it followed her into adulthood. Still, she was able to function at work, and she had what to her was a decent relationship with her husband, who didn't seem to notice her eating habits.

When her daughter was born, Sarah began to realize that she had some unfinished business to deal with from her past. Her scarcity mentality was at odds with her desire to provide a loving environment for her daughter. She found a counselor who helped her connect her secret eating not to food deprivation but to the scarcity of love and acceptance she had experienced from her mother.

She began to realize that, by their behavior, her uncle and her mother had stolen and destroyed things within her that were sacred. When she saw how easy it was to love her own daughter, she struggled to understand why her mother hadn't been able to love and accept her when she was a child.

Somewhere along the course of Sarah's recovery, her mother admitted that her brother had molested her when she was young, and she owned up to the fact that she had withheld love from Sarah. As Sarah continued in her life recovery, she was able to break free from her sense of scarcity and overcome the related negative behaviors. She rose above her life of deceit, self-loathing, confusion, and lack of self-esteem. It took some time, but gradually she began to experience God's gift of abundance in her life.

Life with an Attitude of Scarcity

Any addiction will lead us toward a life of scarcity. We begin to hold on more and more to the scraps that we have collected just to meet some of our basic needs. It becomes a very painful way of life, as we are filled with anxiety and desperation. In many ways, our culture is driven by a scarcity mind-set. A lot of advertising targets this thinking. The folks on Madison Avenue want us to feel as if there might not be enough, so we'll go and buy more just in case.

How do we know whether we are living according to a scarcity mind-set? We begin to take life too seriously. We fear failure, which paradoxically can lead to failure. It's easy to become overly nervous. Our fears block us from the reality of God's gift of abundance.

When we have a scarcity mind-set, we cling to our possessions and even to our toxic relationships, fearing at the same time that we don't deserve them. We live guarded lives that rob us of much of life's richness. And whenever we get frustrated with something in our lives, it's all too easy to fall back into a scarcity mentality.

> When we have a scarcity mind-set, we cling to our possessions and even to our toxic relationships.

The Gift of Abundance Defined

The gift of abundance, on the other hand, leads us to lives filled with new and fulfilling opportunities that we may never have dreamed of or thought possible. The dictionary defines *abundance* as both "a very large quantity of something" and "plentifulness of the good things of life."[1] In recovery, the devastation we experience from living with our problems is replaced with a landscape of blessing upon blessing. We begin to live out the gift of abundance because of the character that emerges from within us as we work the Steps.

Some people may not think that this is a realistic way to approach life. They say it's nothing more than the old "power of positive thinking" model. But we must realize that our individual reality is built on an internal model of how life is. When we live out the scarcity model of life, it is no more real than the abundance model of life. It's how we organize our perceptions. We all become what we think. If we think *scarcity*, we live a life characterized by scarcity. If we think *abundance*, we open ourselves to receiving God's gift of abundance, and we begin to live the abundant life.

The apostle Paul writes, "This same God who takes care of me will supply all your needs from his glorious riches, which have been given to us in Christ Jesus" (Philippians 4:19). That's the promise of the gift of abundance. It is based not on the scarcity of the world around us but on God "glorious riches." Jesus said, "The thief's purpose is to steal and kill and destroy. My purpose is to give them a rich and satisfying life" (John 10:10). We've found that the scarcity model of life is like a thief. It steals, kills, and destroys our

> *If we think abundance, we open ourselves to receiving God's gift of abundance, and we begin to live the abundant life.*

lives. But Jesus came to earth to give us "a rich and satisfying life." The King James Version puts it this way: "I am come that they might have life, and that they might have it more abundantly." It's a promise from God—the gift of abundance!

The Benefits of the Gift of Abundance

One of the primary benefits of an attitude of abundance is that we learn how to appreciate what we have. We can be grateful that we have food, that we have a roof over our heads, that we have friends who walk with us in recovery, and so on. We don't need a lot of money or possessions in order to experience the gift of abundance. It begins with thankfulness for what we already have, no matter how large or small. In fact, it's almost impossible to have a scarcity mentality when we appreciate what we have.

Our attitude of gratitude also leads to a state of generosity in addition to appreciation. Because we appreciate what we have, we develop the habit of giving. This is so much a part of the gift of abundance that, when we are tempted to fall back into scarcity thinking, we can counteract it by giving something away. For example, if we feel that we're lacking recognition for something, we can give recognition to someone else. We cannot live with an attitude of scarcity when we live and act with generosity. Like darkness and light, the two are mutually exclusive.

> When the spirit of scarcity sits on our doorstep tempting us, we need to get together with people who have experienced the gift of abundance.

When the spirit of scarcity sits on our doorstep tempting us, that's a sign that we need to get together with people who have experienced the gift of abundance and let it rub off on us. That's when we need to turn off the TV, stop listening to the news, and go to some recovery meetings. When we are at the meetings, we should share our own stories of how God has brought us out of a scarcity lifestyle into the experience of his gift of abundance.

Finally, as we work through Steps 4, 9, and 10, we mustn't focus on what we've lost. Instead, let's look for the opportunities in each situation. Think of the things that we're leaving behind as part of the old life. We are now moving forward. We give ourselves the freedom to reframe every problem as an opportunity for something new to take place in our lives. We pray and ask God to make that real and to help us experience the gift of abundance he has promised.

The Misstep That Robs Us of the Gift of Abundance

Sometimes we make great progress in experiencing the gifts that God longs to give us. But if at the same time we refuse to release some small thing, it will end up blocking us from experiencing God's abundance. It may not seem small at the time—in fact, in Step 9 we're asked to deal with things that we might refuse to consider. Some things are so damaging that they may seem beyond forgiveness.

The misstep that robs us of the gift of abundance can be stated this way: "Though we can forgive most things, some things are just beyond our ability to forgive." When the hurt has been deep, we often think that by withholding our forgiveness we are protecting ourselves from being hurt again. We think, *If I forgive* that, *then it might happen again!* But it's actually the opposite that usually happens. When we try to protect ourselves by withholding forgiveness, we open ourselves to being hurt again. That's because withholding forgiveness never protects us—it only makes us vulnerable in that area.

It's important to understand that forgiveness is a unilateral process—something we can do by ourselves, regardless of the response or lack of response from the other person. Consequently, we are the ones who benefit from our forgiving. We can truly forgive someone else without being reconciled—or even needing to be reconciled. Reconciliation is a separate process that requires the involvement of both people. Unfortunately, some people stop short of forgiveness because they mistakenly believe they have to be reconciled. Because they don't feel safe enough to pursue reconciliation, they try to protect themselves by withholding forgiveness. But by withholding forgiveness, we only hurt ourselves.

> *Forgiveness is a unilateral process—something we can do by ourselves, regardless of the response or lack of response from the other person.*

To avoid that misunderstanding, we must see that forgiveness and reconciliation are two separate processes. In order for reconciliation to take place, there must be *repentance* on the part of the person being forgiven.

When we withhold forgiveness, it doesn't affect the other person, but it can—and will—affect us. The writer to the Hebrews warns, "Watch out that no poisonous root of bitterness grows up to trouble you, corrupting many" (Hebrews 12:15). In the Contemporary English Version of the Bible, the phrase "corrupting many" is translated as "cause trouble for the rest of you." Not only does bitterness destroy *us*, it destroys others as well. That's because a root of bitterness leads to justifiable resentment.

An attitude of unforgiveness also takes us back to a scarcity mentality. That's why Paul urges us to "get rid of all bitterness, rage, anger, harsh words, and slander, as well as all types of evil behavior. Instead, be kind to each other, tenderhearted, forgiving one another, just as God through Christ has forgiven you" (Ephesians 4:31-32).

How did Christ forgive us? He forgave us "while we were still sinners . . . while we were still his enemies" (Romans 5:8, 10). He forgave us while we were rebellious and set against him. He forgave us when we least deserved it. So our own offering of forgiveness has nothing to do with whether the other person deserves it, wants it, or cares one bit about it. Do you see how freeing that is? *We're* the ones who benefit from our forgiving!

Don't let a spirit of unforgiveness rob you of the gift of abundance.

Unwrapping the Gift of Abundance

1. Describe from your own experience how addiction leads to an attitude of scarcity.

2. Since the beginning of your recovery, what examples can you give of experiencing the gift of abundance?

3. How is forgiveness connected to the gift of abundance?

4. Describe three things that happened to you today for which you are grateful.

7

The Gift of Wisdom

OBVIOUSLY, WHEN WE ARE active in our addictions, wisdom eludes us. Our addictions do not interfere with our intelligence, but they certainly destroy our ability to act wisely. That's why it's so hard for others in our lives to understand how we could do something as stupid as becoming an addict. Common sense, a synonym for wisdom, is absent. We may be streetwise, but that's a survival mechanism unrelated to wisdom.

What's even harder to understand is how the enablers in our lives also seem to lack wisdom. They keep trying to help us by doing the same things that haven't worked before. They believe they are acting wisely, but they are only helping us to stay stuck in our addictions. Many, in their frustration, develop their own addictive behaviors. Amanda is one who paid such a price.

Amanda grew up in a home with an alcoholic mother. Her days were filled with anxiety, and nighttime was chaos. Because she was the eldest, she became her father's helper—which meant she was the primary caretaker in the home, looking after her two younger brothers and caring for her mother as best she could.

That worked until she entered her teens and started finding ways to stay away from home. At school, she was a model student, getting all A's. But outside of school she found some new friends, who loved to party. When she partied, she also discovered sex. At first, when she was partying or having sex with her boyfriend, it seemed she could forget about her home life for a moment. But eventually she had something new to feel anxious about: What if her father found out?

Eventually, even that fear faded as she became

increasingly self-destructive and made all kinds of wrong decisions. She partied more, drank more, and experimented with pot. She married at eighteen, had two abortions, and was divorced by the time she was twenty-two.

During her divorce, she began attending a divorce recovery program at a nearby church. Through the warmth and acceptance of some friends that she made there, she started going to church and was introduced to the saving power of Jesus. One of her new friends also invited her to a codependency meeting, and that started Amanda on a journey of self-discovery. She found that she was a classic enabler.

All of her life had been dedicated to doing things for other people: taking care of her

She was a performer, always checking the audience to measure how well she was doing.

siblings, monitoring her mother, helping her father, even taking care of the needs of her partying friends. In a sense she was a performer, always checking the audience to measure how well she was doing. As long as it appeared that she was performing well, she stayed on the self-made roller coaster of her life.

By this time, she had also started on a strong career path, and her codependency served her well at the office. She felt valued by her boss and her company, but it was all part of her performance mind-set. She was an expert at keeping everyone else happy.

As she continued in her recovery, Amanda found that her life was gradually coming into balance and her need to perform for others was changing. She began journaling, and as she did, she started paying attention to her own needs. It wasn't in a selfish, self-centered way, but she discovered that she could care about other people while also caring about herself. She was finally learning to say *no* in appropriate situations, and she was enjoying a new sense of equilibrium in her relationships.

What surprised her in looking back at her life before recovery was how often she had made bad decisions that had seemed like good decisions at the time. Now, through her relationship with Jesus and by listening to her recovery friends, she was learning how to make better decisions. She was beginning to experience God's gift of wisdom in her life.

Three Types of Wisdom

Through her life recovery program and her involvement in her church community, Amanda learned about three types of wisdom. The first type is *common wisdom* or *secular wisdom*, which may not be true wisdom at all. This was the so-called wisdom of her high school friends. Its basic principle could be summarized as "do what feels good."

In the Bible, after Job has lost his family and all of his possessions and is now afflicted with disease, his wife says to him, "Are you still trying to maintain your integrity? Curse God and die" (Job 2:9). "Give it up," she might have added. "Quit trying so hard." That's common wisdom, and it was much like what Amanda's high school friends had suggested to her. They told her she should forget about her mother's problems and just enjoy the party.

The second type of wisdom can be called *religious wisdom*, which comes from people who try to help us deal with our problems by giving us solutions that sound spiritual but are really just clichés. For Amanda, the input she received from her husband fit into this category. He had been raised in a religiously strict home, and like his father he had a spiritual answer for any of life's problems. But his helpful comments, when analyzed, were much like the comments of Job's friends.

The first friend says, "In the past you have encouraged many people; you have strengthened those who were weak. Your words have supported those who were falling; you encouraged those with shaky knees. But now when trouble strikes, you lose heart. You are terrified when it touches you" (Job 4:3-5).

Job's second friend takes it even further when he says, "Shouldn't someone answer this torrent of words? Is a person proved innocent just by a lot of talking? . . . When you mock God, shouldn't someone make you ashamed? You claim, 'My beliefs are pure, and I am clean in the sight of God.' . . . True wisdom is not a simple matter. Listen! God is doubtless punishing you far less than you deserve!" (Job 11:2-4, 6). In other words, Job, you are being punished because there is sin in your life! A common, simplistic religious answer.

Religious wisdom provides clear and simple answers: "You're suffering because of hidden sin. Just repent and get back on track."

Certainly we may suffer because we have sinned, but not all suffering is caused by our sin. Sometimes we suffer because we have been sinned *against*. Sometimes suffering is just part of being human, or it may be used to glorify God. When Jesus encountered a man who had been blind from birth, his disciples asked whether the man's blindness was caused by his own sin or his parents' sin. Jesus replied, before restoring the man's sight, "This happened so the power of God could be seen in him" (John 9:3).

Not all suffering is caused by our sin. Sometimes we suffer because we have been sinned against.

The third kind of wisdom is *godly wisdom*, which always brings us face-to-face with God's unlimited power, insight, and mercy. At the end of the book of Job, in a section spanning almost four chapters, God displays his wisdom in a series of questions that Job can't answer, all of them designed to stretch Job's understanding of who God is. In the end, Job repents for having too small a picture of God. Godly wisdom always reveals that God is bigger, stronger, and wiser than we are and that he is bigger than simplistic answers to life's troubles.

The Gift of Wisdom Defined

It isn't easy to define the gift of wisdom. At a minimum, it incorporates knowledge, insight, judgment, and good sense. But wisdom is more than simply the sum of its parts.

When God gives us the gift of wisdom, we find that we begin to understand people, things, events, situations, and even ourselves better. We have new insights and new perceptions. You might say that we begin to see people, things, and experiences through God's eyes. And we can transfer our experiences, our knowledge, and our good judgment into godly actions.

> We can transfer our experiences, our knowledge, and our good judgment into godly actions.

When Solomon became Israel's king, God told him that he could ask for anything and God would give it to him. Solomon responded by saying, "Give me wisdom and knowledge to lead [Israel] properly, for who could possibly govern this great people of yours?" (2 Chronicles 1:10). God gave him the gift of wisdom. Today, thankfully, we have the book of Proverbs, which is a compilation of

Solomon's wisdom, including its source: "Fear of the LORD is the foundation of wisdom. Knowledge of the Holy One results in good judgment" (Proverbs 9:10).

In the New Testament, the apostle Paul draws a contrast between secular wisdom and godly wisdom. To him, Jesus Christ represented the wisdom of God. He expounds on this at length in 1 Corinthians, where he writes, "God has united you with Christ Jesus. For our benefit God made him to be wisdom itself" (1 Corinthians 1:30). In Colossians 2:3, he adds, "In [Jesus] lie hidden all the treasures of wisdom and knowledge," and he later writes, "Let the message about Christ, in all its richness, fill your lives. Teach and counsel each other with all the wisdom he gives" (Colossians 3:16). The gift of godly wisdom is given to those who truly know Christ. The more we grow in our relationship with Jesus, the more we experience his wisdom.

Developing the Gift of Wisdom

What do we do when we're given the gift of wisdom? It doesn't come wrapped in a neat little package. We've never met anyone who entered into life recovery with wisdom as the motivation. Like Amanda, most people enter into recovery after a long period of confusion and self-reliance. At the beginning, the whole purpose of life recovery is to stop the pain. As we let the light of God penetrate our lives, we find that the gift of wisdom needs to be nurtured and developed. But how do we become wise?

Wisdom begins by sincerely seeking God's will and wanting to carry it out. Daily prayer and meditation create a mature spirituality. As God's truth and presence seep into our lives, wisdom-based living replaces futile home remedies and attempts to be smart enough or strong enough to overcome our struggles.

Godly wisdom is a combination of the depth of our relationship with God and our ability to bring our experiences into relationship with him.

We will find that godly wisdom is a combination of the depth of our relationship with God and our ability to bring our experiences into relationship with him. Because self-awareness is part of the process, we must become increasingly truthful about our own flawed humanness. How else can we develop a healthy self-awareness? We do this by paying attention to our thoughts, emotions, and experiences, asking God to help us see the truth about ourselves. In the process, we develop a wisdom that is born of God and of knowing ourselves better. "We may think ourselves clever in our self-delusion," writes Cheryl Eckl, "but only the truthful are wise."[1]

The Misstep That Robs Us of the Gift of Wisdom

There is a false wisdom that is born of pride. Solomon helps us when he says, "Pride leads to disgrace, but with humility comes wisdom" (Proverbs 11:2). When we fully surrender to God in our recovery, we indicate by that act that we have become willing to do whatever it takes to change our lives. But pride is subtle. As we begin to do better, we can be tempted to continue in our own self-sufficient wisdom. The misstep is often articulated like this: "Because I'm doing so well in recovery, I don't need additional counseling, meetings, or even medication." We forget that our self-sufficiency is what perpetuated our problems and troubles prior to our recovery.

Our pride can also cut us off from those who need us in order to take the next step in their own recovery. Pride can make us feel as if we don't want to be bothered. Research on recovery points out that the two most important principles that prevent relapse are that God has become a reality in our lives, and that we continue our own recovery by helping others. Taking Step 12 seriously is an essential part of our continuing to recover from our issues.

Just as important is that we continue to reach out to others for our own ongoing recovery. It is pride once again that stops us there. We may feel that it's a sign of weakness to continue reaching out for additional help, but we need to remember that it took a humble willingness to start our recovery in the first place, and it takes a humble willingness to continue in our recovery.

Unwrapping the Gift of Wisdom

1. Describe a time when you experienced each of the three types of wisdom—secular, religious, and godly.

2. How would you describe the difference between godly wisdom and religious wisdom?

3. How does pride destroy true wisdom?

4. How does seeking to do God's will lead to the experience of the gift of wisdom?

8

The Gift of Self-Control

IT'S AMAZING HOW we can fool ourselves into thinking we are in control, when in reality we are being controlled. The alcohol is in control—or the drugs, the gambling, the shopping, the cutting, the pornography. We fool ourselves mainly because no one knows our secret. You've probably heard the saying that "we are as sick as our secrets." But most addicts don't agree. It's almost as if they're saying, "As long as no one finds out, I am in control."

Bill pastored a small suburban church, and his

parishioners loved him. He was married to Lisa and they had two young boys. The church had no staff except for a part-time secretary, who was in the office only in the mornings, so Bill spent a lot of afternoons in the church office alone, supposedly working on his sermon. What the people of the church didn't know was that, much of the time, Bill was actually looking at pornography. He had been addicted since seeing his first porn when he was nine years old. Still, he lived with the lie to himself that he was in control.

He was good at keeping it hidden. No one had the password to his computer, and no one would have suspected anything anyway. He was careful not to look at porn when he was at home, so Lisa had no idea what was going on either.

One afternoon, Bill felt bored with looking at pictures and watching videos, and he decided to check out what was going on in some of the chat rooms. That brought back the excitement, and soon he had several special female friends he chatted with. The conversations became very sexually explicit. Of course, no one in the chat room knew his real name, and no one knew he was a pastor. Gradually, he began to spend more time talking with one woman in particular, and they became convinced they had developed a strong attraction to each other, even though it was all based on false information and they had never met.

One time, his new lady friend suggested that he call her directly and gave him her cell phone number. Soon Bill's afternoons were spent engaging in sex talk with "Samantha" and masturbating. Eventually, they left behind the false identities; Bill now knew he was talking with Evelyn, and Evelyn knew she was talking with Bill, though she still had no idea that he was a pastor.

At the end of one conversation, Evelyn suggested that Bill come and see her. They lived more than a thousand miles apart, but that wasn't a problem to Evelyn. She offered to pay for Bill's airline ticket, and soon the plan became a reality. Bill told Lisa that he was visiting a church that had expressed some interest in calling him to be their pastor, and that satisfied Lisa for the moment.

But when Bill was on his third visit with Evelyn, Lisa got suspicious and called the church where he was supposedly interviewing. They had never heard of Bill. Frightened now, Lisa sprang into action. She spent more than an hour in Bill's office trying different passwords and finally got into his computer. She was devastated by what she found. Ten years of trusting her husband suddenly vanished as she sat there in shock.

Bill came to grips with the fact that what he had thought he had under control was actually controlling him.

Lisa decided that she would not contact Bill to tell him what she had found. Instead, she called the denomination's district superintendent to ask for help. When Bill arrived home, he was met by his wife, the chairman of the church board, and the district superintendent, and they had a hastily prepared intervention with Bill. Caught by the facts, Bill admitted to everything he had done and agreed to enter a treatment program for sexual addiction. In that program, Bill came to grips with the fact that what he had thought he had under control was actually controlling him.

Many afternoons at the church, he had sat in his office weeping, knowing that, if he were found out, it would destroy his image and devastate his wife. He confessed his sinfulness to God and begged him for forgiveness. But nothing really changed. He might stay away from the pornography for a day or two at the most, but it seemed as if he couldn't stop himself. "It just happened," he once said in his Twelve Step group.

He kept asking himself, "Why doesn't God just take away the desire from me?" The answer is that God won't do for us something that we need to do for ourselves. But when we are actively dealing with our addictions, God often gives us a gift—the gift of self-control, which is a fruit of the Holy Spirit—although it isn't something he'll give us without our participation. We must be actively at work in our life recovery.

> *The gift of self-control only emerges when we are in relationship with other people.*

The Gift of Self-Control

Bill's life had become so out of control that he was almost relieved when his addiction was uncovered. His lies were unmasked, especially his lies to himself. For so long, Bill's isolation had given him a false sense of self-control. Now he began to experience the reality that the gift of self-control only emerges when we are in relationship with other people. If we isolate ourselves, any self-control we think we have begins to fail.

When we think we can do it alone, we discover the truth of Proverbs 5:22-23: "An evil man is held captive by his own sins; they are ropes that catch and hold him. He will die for lack of self-control; he will be lost because of his great foolishness." Another proverb tells us that it is "better to have self-control than to conquer a city" (Proverbs 16:32). When we are caught in the web of an addiction or any destructive behavior, whatever self-control we experience is always a temporary state. It requires the gift of self-control to bring true and lasting change, and that is what life recovery is all about.

Self-control is defined as "the ability to control oneself, in particular one's emotions and desires, especially in difficult situations."[1] Another definition involves the idea of being able to restrain our emotions or our actions. We typically connect self-control to the strength of our willpower. But that's a false assumption.

The Powerlessness of Willpower

It is an astounding paradox that, when we finally come to grips with the reality that willpower is worthless, control of ourselves begins to become a reality. Willpower is not what it's cracked up to be. Willpower will eventually run out of power.

Willpower runs out of power because it is based in our conscious mind, which controls only about 5 percent of what we do. The other 95 percent is controlled by our subconscious mind, which is like the hard drive of a computer. For years it has been programmed for certain behaviors, and it is not easily reprogrammed. You might recall a time when you were driving home and were in a deep conversation with someone else in the car. Remember how it felt when you were suddenly home? Did you ask yourself, "How did we get here?" Because you were so intensely involved in your conversation (which had the attention of your conscious mind), you didn't remember anything about the trip home—but your subconscious mind did the driving for you, and it did a great job.

Another way to understand the subconscious is to think about what happens when we walk somewhere. Unless we have a physical disability, we don't even think about walking—we just walk. But watch a toddler as he or she learns to walk. It's an awkward, tentative, and difficult process; but gradually the subconscious mind begins to connect different neurons in the brain, and walking becomes more natural until it's automatic.

The same thing happens in any process addiction, such as Bill's addiction to pornography. When we start a behavior, it is under the control of our conscious mind. But the more we repeat and practice that behavior, the more neurons regarding that behavior are wired together in our brains. Soon there is a well-worn neural path that simply takes over, and the conscious mind is powerless to break the pattern on its own. We need recovery.

The Gift of Self-Control

The apostle Paul lists *self-control* as part of the fruit we will experience in our lives when we surrender to the Holy Spirit. Peter describes where self-control fits into our recovery when he writes, "Make every effort to respond to God's promises. Supplement your faith with a generous provision of moral excellence, and moral excellence with knowledge, and knowledge with self-control, and self-control with patient endurance, and patient endurance with godliness, and godliness with brotherly affection,

and brotherly affection with love for everyone"
(2 Peter 1:5-7). We need to respond to all of God's
gifts and promises. As we do, not only do we receive
his gifts, but his gifts also lead
us onward to the ability to love
everyone whom God has placed
in our lives.

The gift of self-control changes our orientation: Instead of seeking to accomplish our own will, we desire to understand God's will for us.

As we seek to improve our
conscious awareness of God
through prayer and meditation,
the gift of self-control changes
our orientation: Instead of seeking to accomplish our own will,
we desire to understand God's will
for us. The more our desire to do God's will overrules
our own will, the more our experience of self-control
grows. It's not our willpower that does it; it is God's
gift to us in our recovery.

The Misstep That Robs Us of the Gift of Self-Control

There is a common misstep that can quickly rob
us of the gift of self-control. It is tied to our willpower. We tell ourselves that we will change . . .
tomorrow. Every time Bill watched pornography on

his computer, he told himself it was the last time. Tomorrow would be a new beginning. Each time he hung up from his sexual conversations with Evelyn, he was filled with guilt and shame, and he would declare that tomorrow would be different—this would be his last call to her!

The apostle James understood this pattern of promising to make changes in our lives tomorrow. He writes, "How do you know what your life will be like tomorrow? Your life is like the morning fog—it's here a little while and then it's gone. What you ought to say is, 'If the Lord wants us to, we will live and do this or that.' Otherwise you are boasting about your own pretentious plans, and all such boasting is evil. Remember, it is sin to know what to do and then not do it" (James 4:14-17). Paul asserts the same thing when he tells the Colossians, "*Now* is the time to get rid of anger, rage, malicious behavior, slander, and dirty language. Don't lie to each other, for you have stripped off your old sinful nature and all its wicked deeds. Put on your new nature, and be renewed as you learn to know your Creator and become like him" (Colossians 3:8-10, italics added).

Tomorrow has no power to initiate change in our lives today. *Now* is where all the power is. Waiting even one more day is a decision to stay on a path that has proved to be destructive. Nothing begins tomorrow. It can only begin today. The gift of self-control is not available tomorrow. It only functions in the here and now. Make today a new day in which your actions and responses will be an expression of God's gift of self-control.

> Tomorrow has no power to initiate change in our lives today. Now *is where all the power is.*

Unwrapping the Gift of Self-Control

1. How does the excuse of "it just happens" divert us from the reality of our lack of self-control?

2. If self-control is a gift, how do we develop it?

3. How does the attitude of "I can quit tomorrow" reveal a lack of self-control?

4. How is self-control different from willpower?

9

The Gift of Courage

IN THE SERENITY PRAYER, we ask God for courage to change the things we can. It takes courage to make major changes in our lives. Sometimes it even takes courage to change a small part of our lives. And it takes courage to stop our denial, face reality, and get help. That little bit of courage at the beginning of our recovery can set the stage for our receiving the gift of courage later on. That's what Rich found to be true.

Rich is a lawyer who had a love for red wine. He typically could down an entire bottle all by himself and still appear to function normally. No one seemed concerned about how much he drank because they didn't see that it had any great effect on his behavior. But gradually the "one bottle a day" started to stretch until it was two bottles a day. Then it spiraled completely out of control until all that Rich seemed to want was a bottle of red wine at each mealtime—forget the food—and another bottle for an in-between-meal snack.

When Rich's fiancée came over in the evenings to cook for him—"so he'd at least get some nourishment"—he was typically not in the mood for food. "I ate something during the day," he'd say as he took another drink and brushed away her concerns.

For a while, she even went to the store to buy his wine for him—"so he wouldn't be out there driving." But finally she gave up and stayed away. Watching Rich destroy himself was just too painful.

Eventually, someone suggested she go to an Al-Anon meeting. When she did, she began to recognize Rich's behavior as typically alcoholic. She also saw herself as a classic enabler, and she became determined to no longer try to change Rich, but to change herself instead.

Meanwhile, Rich had begun to realize that he was in trouble. By then, he not only didn't know how to stop drinking, he was afraid to stop. He had consumed at least four bottles of wine each day for the past two weeks, and he was aware of the potential physical consequences of stopping cold turkey. Still, at some level he knew

She saw herself as a classic enabler, and she became determined to change.

he couldn't continue like this. Finally, he decided to call an acquaintance whom he knew was a recovering alcoholic. They weren't close, mostly because Rich was ashamed to admit he had a problem, but Don was the only one he thought he could ask for help. When Rich called, Don said he'd be right over. When he saw the condition that Rich was in, he loaded him up in his car and drove him to the hospital.

The doctors immediately started to medically detox Rich. Several days later, he willingly admitted himself to the hospital's treatment program. As he sobered up, he realized how close he had come to totally messing up his life. He had finally scared himself enough that he was ready to make changes in his life. Because helping other alcoholics recover was part of Don's own recovery, he became a regular visitor as Rich went through the thirty-day program—and beyond.

The Courage of Recovery

It took courage for Rich to call Don for help. They were both attorneys, but they weren't close as friends, mostly because of Rich. He knew that Don was a recovering alcoholic, and he didn't like being around "those recovery people." Today, Rich and Don are good friends, and both are continuing in their recovery. In fact, Don became Rich's first sponsor, and today Rich still expresses his thanks to Don for saving his life.

Shame is the destroyer, not only of recovery but also of courage. The apostle John writes in his first letter, "Dear children, remain in fellowship with Christ so that when he returns, you will be full of courage and not shrink back from him in shame" (1 John 2:28). When we have the gift of courage, we overcome our shame. Rich had to overcome the shame of his condition before he could find the courage to call Don. But first he had to come to the point where he felt he had no choice. He knew that, if he didn't do something to change his circumstances, he would literally die. So the life-and-death situation allowed him to overcome his shame and reach out with courage. Sadly, most of us have to come to our end of ourselves before we ask God to give us the courage to change. That's why an intervention can often hasten the beginning of recovery and reduce the risk of dying.

> Most of us have to come to our end of ourselves before we ask God to give us the courage to change.

The Gift of Courage Defined

A simple definition of courage is "the ability to do something that frightens [us]."[1] That was Rich's experience. He was able to call for help because he feared dealing with his alcoholism less than he feared dying from his alcohol consumption. But it nonetheless took courage to call Don. Another definition of courage is "doing what needs to be done, when it needs to be done, no matter the cost."

Before we started in our recovery, we typically refused to do what needed to be done. In the back of our minds, we knew we couldn't continue the way we were living. It was miserable. But we procrastinated on getting started with the necessary changes. We had all kinds of false starts as we kept trying to fix everything our own way. We didn't want the pain or the work of recovery, so we put it off in an attempt to avoid the deeper pain of changing.

Finally the pain of staying in the midst of our struggles became more painful than what we imagined we would face in confronting our problems. We became aware that it had to be done, no matter the cost. Nelson Mandela once said, "I learned that courage was not the absence of fear, but the triumph over it. . . . The brave man is not he who does not feel afraid, but he who conquers that fear."[2] We don't wait for the fear to go away—it won't. To succeed in life recovery, we must confront our fear and conquer it. By God's gift of courage, we can succeed!

The Benefits of the Gift of Courage

As we continue in our life recovery and it takes hold, our actions become governed by an awareness of who we are as children of God. Increasingly, we have the attitude that Paul writes about in Romans 8:31: "If God is for us, who can ever be against us?"

What a contrast to our old way of thinking! No

longer do we walk around feeling that everyone is against us or that we had better do whatever it takes to defend ourselves, our rights, and our ground. There may still be some people we have hurt who might still be against us, but when we realize that God is really for us, we have the courage to make amends.

> *When we realize that God is really for us, we have the courage to make amends.*

What a gift to realize that we are doing some pretty difficult things as part of our life recovery. We wade right in. We work through Steps 4 and 5, taking a fearless inventory and confessing our wrongs to God and to another person. That takes courage! When it comes to the difficult step of making amends where we have hurt others, we no longer avoid doing what is right.

We solve problems rather than avoiding them or hoping they will get better on their own. We move forward in our journey through the Steps, no matter the price or the difficulty. As a result, we not only experience the gift of courage but also grow in our feelings of worth and value as we see that our character defects are being replaced with positive traits. We become aware that our most humiliating defect—cowardice—is fading. God is replacing it with courage!

It's important to realize that the gift of courage goes beyond the courage to work our way through life recovery. That's an important part of the gift, but it's not all of it. Courage goes much further. Whatever our addictions—whether they were chemical addictions, such as alcohol or drugs; or process addictions, such as sexual addiction, gambling, or shopping—they were designed to help us hide from life. Instead of facing life's challenges, we hid behind our addictions. That's a coward's way to live. What's exciting about the gift of courage is that it replaces our old cowardice with boldness, strength, and initiative.

The gift of courage replaces our old cowardice with boldness, strength, and initiative.

We see the gift of courage at work in us as we deal more effectively with our relationships, jobs, finances, and health. We now face these issues head-on. We don't need to hide from life anymore. Instead, we have the boldness to live life courageously.

As we continue in our life recovery, we are increasingly able to stand with Joshua in being "strong and courageous" (Joshua 1:6). We also respond willingly to Paul's exhortation in 1 Corinthians 16:13: "Be on guard. Stand firm in the faith. Be courageous. Be strong." Life is not meant to be *endured* by just getting by. We are called to live courageously. As we surrender our life recovery to God, he gives us the gift of courage. Now let's exercise our gift!

The Misstep That Robs Us of the Gift of Courage

As we develop the gift of courage and feel better equipped to deal with life's problems, we must be careful not to allow ourselves to slip back into old patterns. It's easy to forget how far God has brought us and what he has given us, and instead to start thinking that staying the course in our recovery is up to us. One of the missteps we can take is to think that, because God has forgiven us, we don't need to go back and rehash what we've done. "Isn't it enough that we've dealt with God about these issues? Why not leave the past in the past?" we ask ourselves.

But unfinished issues are not confined to the past. They will continue to express themselves in the present, so in fact they are present issues. If we only confess them to God, by God's own standards they are unfinished. His instruction is to "confess your sins to each other and pray for each other so that you may be healed" (James 5:16). One cannot escape the "each other" injunction in that passage.

The early church was healthy because believers met together, confessed their sins to each other, and prayed for each other.

The early church was healthy because believers followed the principle of mutual confession. They met together, confessed their sins to each other, and prayed for each other. But somewhere along the way, the church became more organized and the principle changed to "confess your sin to God and to your priest." Then came the Protestant Reformation, and the reformers did away with confessing to the priest. Instead, we were left with confessing our sins to God alone. As a result, we lost something important in our Christian life—and it made us weaker. God knew the importance of confession when he had James write these words—we are to confess our sins to each other.

That's why Step 5 tells us to share the results of our fearless moral inventory with God, with ourselves, and with another human being. That's where the power of change resides. Yes, God has forgiven us if we have confessed and have changed our ways. But he clearly instructs us not to stop with confessing to him. When we open up to other people, it connects us, keeps us humble, grounds us in reality, and leads to healing. That's the promise of the gift of courage.

Unwrapping the Gift of Courage

1. Why is change so difficult?

2. In what ways does recovery require courage?

3. How does unfinished business rob us of the gift of courage?

4. How would you explain passivity as a lack of courage?

10

The Gift of Happiness

EVERYBODY WANTS TO BE HAPPY. The problem is that so many of us make happiness the object of our search, not realizing that true happiness is never found by searching for it; it is always a by-product of a certain kind of living. When we think that something or some person will make us happy, we will soon realize that true happiness still eludes us. Then there are those times when we find ourselves immersed in something enjoyable or meaningful, and we suddenly realize we have just had an experience of happiness.

In our search for happiness, we often think something like this: *Maybe* this *will make me happy. Maybe* this *is what I've been needing to help me relax*. Such thoughts should be a warning that we are on the wrong track and could be headed for trouble. That's how Mark got started.

Several months into his recovery, Mark began to realize that he had started to use pornography as a way to soothe himself. He had grown up in a family that based everything on performance. His older brother always seemed able to handle the family stress; but Mark experienced a lot of anxiety as a kid, and it didn't get any better for him as an adult.

In about the ninth grade, Mark and a couple of his friends discovered pornography. When he spent time looking at the images and masturbating, he found that his overall anxiety would lessen for a while. He felt guilty when his obsession expanded, thanks to the Internet, but he rationalized it by focusing on the fact that for a while he felt less anxious.

What he hadn't counted on, however, was that his anxiety began to be replaced by out-of-control anger. During his high school years, he regularly got into fights, and pornography became a temporary release from his anger.

When he got married, he thought that having sex with his wife would replace his desire for pornography, but it didn't. (It never does.) In fact, because pornography gave him a feeling of control, it remained his go-to stress reliever. But his anger was becoming a problem in his marriage.

He felt guilty when his obsession expanded, but he rationalized it by focusing on the fact that for a while he felt less anxious.

Some men turn to alcohol to relieve stress; some turn to sex and pornography; and others displace their anger by "kicking the dog." Over time, Mark found that he was doing all three. When his wife uncovered his pornography addiction, Mark went into recovery. As he dealt with his pornography addiction and his issues with alcohol, he gradually realized that he was still not a happy man. Though he would continue to recover from his addictions, he also needed to get into counseling to deal with his anger.

His counselor, who was also in recovery, suggested that Mark do some Step 4 work on his issues with his father. At first, he didn't understand. He thought things were fine now between himself and his father. His counselor pointed out to him the importance of looking at his childhood relationship with his father.

It took some time, but Mark gradually began to remember things. One of the first issues he encountered was how much he had feared his father as a young boy. He had always been critical of himself for feeling that fear and had tried to put it out of his mind, but as he worked on remembering, this memory was the first to jump out at him. As he started to understand himself and his childhood reactions to his father, he began to see that much of his anger was connected to these issues.

Over time, Mark began to see clearly how his relationship with his father had affected his sense of masculinity. He also began to see something deep down inside that he was afraid to admit: He was angry about things his father had done to him and about things his father had never done with him that he had longed to share with his father.

As Mark continued in his life recovery journey and followed through with his counselor, his anger became much more controllable. When his counselor took him to the point where he was able to forgive his father, it was as if Mark had finally started to feel alive. The happiness he had longed for but could never experience became a by-

The happiness he had longed for but could never experience became a by-product of his counseling and recovery.

product of his counseling and recovery. By forgiving his father, Mark gained a new perspective on his own life and happiness.

The Gift of Happiness Defined

We all seem to know whether we are happy or not, and we may even feel that we have a right to be happy. After all, our inalienable rights are "life, liberty, and the pursuit of happiness." So we pursue happiness, only to find that it always seems to elude us.

But we never give up the chase. We think that happiness is something we must search for. We need to "find" happiness, regardless of the cost. Couples divorce because they think that finding a new mate will make them happy—as if being with the "right" person will bring happiness. But like so many things in life, true happiness does not result from casting about for an easy solution.

In defining the word *happy*, the dictionary uses terms such as "feeling or showing pleasure or contentment," "satisfied," and "having a sense of confidence in."[1] Happiness can also be defined as a state of mind that results from a positive attitude.

Although not everyone is born with a sunny, optimistic disposition, no one has to settle for a pessimistic, dreary outlook on life. Enjoying the gift of happiness is not for only certain people. Anyone can find significance, contentment, and satisfaction in life. Happiness is a gift given to all who make up their minds that they will enjoy life to the fullest.

The Promise of Happiness

The world promises everything and often leaves us with nothing but regret and despair. Some would say that happiness is a choice we make, and there's some truth to that; but life often makes it very difficult to choose happiness. But there is a rich happiness that is produced when we live godly lives and pursue a godly path. "The hopes of the godly result in happiness, but the expectations of the wicked come to nothing" (Proverbs 10:28). The psalmist echoes this promise: "Make me walk along the path of your commands, for that is where my happiness is found" (Psalm 119:35). And King David assures us that God is the source of our happiness: "Give me happiness, O Lord, for I give myself to you" (Psalm 86:4).

There is a rich happiness that is produced when we live godly lives and pursue a godly path.

Some people go through their entire lives desiring happiness but never achieving it. In life recovery, we find that, when our hope is based on God, it leads to godly living, which then leads to happiness. As our hearts become more and more in tune with the heart of God, we experience the gift of happiness as a by-product of a godly life.

In our recovery, we will go through the same learning process as the apostle Paul, who ultimately discovered the secret of true contentment: "I have learned how to be content with whatever I have. I know how to live on almost nothing or with everything. I have learned the secret of living in every situation, whether it is with a full stomach or empty, with plenty or little. For I can do everything through Christ, who gives me strength" (Philippians 4:11-13). This is the result of receiving and experiencing the gift of happiness. In these verses, Paul defines happiness as a deep contentment rooted in our faith in Christ. We can never buy happiness or find it by searching. It is simply a gift from God.

Some of the happiest people in the world are those who have surrendered their lives to Jesus Christ, even though from a material standpoint they have little or nothing in this life. Likewise, there are many happy people in recovery who may have lost everything they had—career, income, family, status—but through their recovery have found the true source of happiness: God. True happiness can best be described as *being content with whatever we have.*

The Misstep that Robs Us of the Gift of Happiness

One of the possible missteps along the road to recovery is deciding to keep our old, addictive friends. We can even spiritualize this behavior by saying, "Because Jesus would want me to help my old friends, I don't need to change where I go or who I hang out with." Recovering alcoholics think they can hang out with their old friends at the bar and not relapse. Recovering sex addicts think they can still exchange pornographic jokes and pictures by e-mail. "After all," they rationalize, "if I don't keep in touch with my friends, how can I help them?"

Paul told his young protégé Timothy to "run from anything that stimulates youthful lusts. Instead, pursue righteous living, faithfulness, love, and peace. Enjoy the companionship of those who call on the Lord with pure hearts" (2 Timothy 2:22). We can stay available to our old friends for when they need help, but when we're tempted to act as if old times won't pull us down, we need to do what Paul told Timothy: *Run!*

> "Run from anything that stimulates youthful lusts. Instead, pursue righteous living, faithfulness, love, and peace."
>
> *(2 Timothy 2:22)*

The Bible is clear that we need to avoid people and places that would tempt us to fall back into our old ways. Paul is also the one who warned the Corinthians: "If you think you are standing strong, be careful not to fall" (1 Corinthians 10:12). We can't afford the arrogance of thinking we can handle those old patterns. We have habit pathways established in our brains that can trigger behaviors before we can think—and suddenly we've fallen, relapsed.

It's not just a matter of avoiding the old people and places. We need to replace those contacts with "the companionship of those who call on the Lord with pure hearts." In order to change the habit pathways in our brains, we must build new, stronger pathways that keep us focused on our recovery. We do this by replacing the people we spend time with. That's partly why we go to meetings even when we are feeling stronger. We need to spend time with people who not only understand what's involved in life recovery but who are also on the same path that we are.

There's a reason why Step 12 is the last step. It's only when we are stronger in our own recovery that we can be available to others. It's important that we get involved with others in recovery, but our help must be anchored in our own long-term success in recovery.

Jude ends his letter in the New Testament by urging his readers to be helpful but also to exercise caution. He writes, "You must show mercy to those whose faith is wavering. Rescue others by snatching them from the flames of judgment. Show mercy to still others, but do so with great caution, hating the sins that contaminate their lives" (Jude 1:22-23).

It's important that we get involved with others in recovery, but our help must be anchored in our own long-term success in recovery.

It's easy to apply his words to Step 12: "Show mercy to those who have relapsed. Rescue others from the flames of their addiction. Show mercy to those still in the grip of their addiction. But do so with great caution so you don't contaminate your own recovery."

Unwrapping the Gift of Happiness

1. How do our past unresolved relational problems rob us of the gift of happiness?

2. If happiness is a by-product of other things, what are some things that can lead us to experience the gift of happiness?

3. How would you compare *happiness* with *contentment*? How does one find contentment?

4. How is running from old problems and relationships a part of experiencing the gift of happiness?

11

The Gift of Serenity

THE ORIGINAL SERENITY PRAYER IS much longer than the one we regularly repeat in our recovery meetings, which incorporates only the first two stanzas. In the next part of the prayer, we are encouraged to live life one day at a time and to accept that life has its hardships. We can all acknowledge that there are many things in life that we cannot change. But we can experience the gift of serenity when we surrender our lives to God and trust that he will "make all things right."[1]

There is also a *false* serenity that can divert our attention from our issues and temporarily give us the illusion that we are really on track. If we aren't careful, this diversion can easily set us up for a relapse. Allen was someone who needed to be careful, for he was in danger of derailing his recovery.

Allen was a twenty-nine-year-old alcoholic who had been in recovery for three years. He had thirty months of sobriety—though in many ways, he had simply switched addictions from being an alcoholic to being codependent.

At the treatment center he met Betsy, and it didn't take long for him to get involved in helping her deal with her drug addiction. He was one of those addicts who jumps quickly to Step 12, thinking that it's part of his own recovery. But he wasn't ready for Step 12 in that way. And even though he was helpful to Betsy, it was really a way for him to avoid dealing with his own life issues. And even though he wouldn't admit it to his sponsor, he had gotten emotionally involved with Betsy as well.

Let's count the ways that Allen was *not* recovering. Since becoming sober, he had lost his apartment and was living with another recovering alcoholic. His car had been repossessed, and he had to get around on his bicycle. He was fired from his job and struggled with a part-time job that didn't pay enough for him to get his own place. All of this happened after he got sober and started in recovery.

He was serious about recovering from his alcoholism. He had a sponsor, who was after him to get another job, even if it were a second part-time job working at a fast-food place. He didn't tell his sponsor about Betsy, nor did he mention that working full-time wouldn't leave him enough time to help Betsy, his "recovery project."

Allen said that he was serious about working on Step 4 (taking a fearless moral inventory); but his progress was slow, and he hadn't shared anything with his sponsor. In essence, he had worked the first three Steps and then skipped the rest so he could help Betsy. In terms of how he was dealing with the rest of his life, he was just as irresponsible as he had been when he was drinking.

If we were to grade Allen on his recovery, we might give him a B for his progress in dealing with his alcoholism; but he would get a D or an F for his lack of progress in the rest of his life. He had surrendered his drinking, but he still thought he could control everything else. He thought that recovery was only about his addiction. He hadn't yet discovered *life* recovery. Consequently, he still lived in chaos, moving from one crisis to the next. True recovery is meant to touch *every* aspect of our lives.

The Gift of Serenity Defined

Serenity is not easy to define. Some might try to describe it in terms of what's *not* there—the absence of agitation, stress, or anxiety. If that were the meaning of serenity, no one would ever experience it. When are we ever stress free, or worry free, or not feeling even a bit of anxiety? But the truth is, even in the midst of life's problems, we can experience the gift of serenity.

> He had surrendered his drinking, but he still thought he could control everything else. He thought that recovery was only about his addiction.

The best way to define serenity is to look at three key words in the Serenity Prayer that define the state of composure we seek. Those words are *acceptance*, *courage*, and *wisdom*.

We experience the gift of serenity when we can

accept what we cannot change, have the courage to change what we can, and the wisdom to know the difference. Let's look more closely at each word.

When we experience the gift of serenity, we learn to accept our past.

Acceptance is the willingness to take what life offers us and make the best of it. Some things that we experience we would never *choose*— they are just a part of life. But we don't merely resign ourselves to the inevitable. Along with acceptance, there is also a *welcoming*, as when we welcome a new daughter-in-law or son-in-law into the family.

When we experience the gift of serenity, we learn to accept our past. There's nothing we can do, apart from asking or extending forgiveness and making amends, that will change the reality of our past. This means we accept our childhood experiences, the relationship we had with our parents and siblings, and the mistakes we made when we were active in our addiction. All of these are part of the past and cannot be changed, only accepted. And acceptance brings with it serenity.

The second word—*courage*—suggests that we

take action because there are some things we *can* change. It takes courage to face our addictions and begin the recovery process. It takes courage to undertake our fearless moral inventory and to make amends to those we have hurt. And it takes courage to take responsibility for our lives.

Courage is an attitude that works in the here-and-now. I may have courage to face my past or my future, but both of those actions are in the present. Today is the only day when I can exercise courage. As the full Serenity Prayer affirms, serenity comes from "living one day at a time."

Finally, *wisdom*. Serenity doesn't come from knowledge; it comes from seeking wisdom. The source of all wisdom is God. You may have noticed that two of the three concepts that define serenity are also gifts of life recovery. As we seek to experience the gift of serenity, we exercise two other gifts that we have already received: courage and wisdom.

The wisdom to know the difference between the things we cannot change (acceptance) and the things we can (courage) is probably the most difficult part of the serenity equation. But if we are willing to accept what can't be changed and to have the courage to take action on what can be changed, God will give us the wisdom to discern the difference. Wisdom becomes easier as we seek to do the will of God.

The Source of Serenity

Serenity is a gift of life recovery, given to us by God. The source of serenity is God himself, and we experience his gift when we seek to follow his will, not our own will. According to Step 11, we will find serenity when we seek to know God's will through prayer and meditation and then pray for the power to carry out God's will in our lives. Proverbs 3:5-6 tells us, "Trust in the LORD with all your heart; do not depend on your own understanding. Seek his will in all you do, and he will show you which path to take." God's path is the path of serenity.

When we pursue God's will—not our own—and ask him for the power to live it out, we receive his gift of serenity.

Prior to our recovery, most of our prayers consisted of asking God to do something for us— give to us, forgive us, bless us, fix us, protect us. It was all about what *we* wanted. We were seeking the fulfillment of our own will. Serenity comes when we seek *God's* will. When we pursue his will—not our own—and ask him for the power to live it out, we receive his gift of serenity.

There is another ingredient to finding serenity: discovering how much we are loved by God. For years, while mired in our addictions, we were probably very angry with God because it didn't seem as if he cared for us. After all, he wasn't doing what we asked him to do. Because we were seeking our own will, when God didn't respond, we dismissed him as unconcerned about our lives.

But in recovery we find that, as we seek to know God's will, we also grow in our experience of his love for us—a love so great that the apostle Paul was inspired to write these words: "I am convinced that nothing can ever separate us from God's love. Neither death nor life, neither angels nor demons, neither our fears for today nor our worries about tomorrow—not even the powers of hell can separate us from God's love" (Romans 8:38). Wow! Paul says there is nothing in all the universe that can make God stop loving us. There is nothing that anyone else can do, or that we ourselves can do, that will stop God from loving us. Knowing that we are loved so unconditionally is part of what brings us the gift of serenity.

The Misstep That Robs Us of the Gift of Serenity

Some Twelve Step groups restrict people from talking about Jesus. When we give in to the demands of a secularized group, we participate in restricting everyone from freely expressing their experience of Step 11. (What about those people who, in seeking through prayer and meditation to improve their conscious contact with God, find Jesus?) But an even worse misstep is to use that restriction as an excuse to stop attending a Twelve Step group. By withdrawing from such a group, we may reduce our agitation, but we are not acting with courage. We may be missing an opportunity to share what God is doing in our lives.

The problem may be in how we respond or how we share our faith. Are we preaching instead of simply sharing our experience? When we share our faith in Jesus based on our practice of Step 11, we're more likely to find that people are open to what we are sharing. If that openness doesn't occur, it becomes part of our Serenity Prayer as we ask God to help us accept what we can't change.

> *God, grant me the serenity*
> *to accept the things I cannot change;*
> *courage to change the things I can;*
> *and wisdom to know the difference.*
>
> *Living one day at a time;*
> *enjoying one moment at a time;*
> *accepting hardships as the pathway to peace;*
> *taking, as Jesus did, this sinful world,*
> *as it is, not as I would have it.*
>
> *Trusting that God will make all things right,*
> *if I surrender to his will;*
> *so that I may be reasonably happy in this life,*
> *and supremely happy with him forever*
> *in the next.*
> *Amen.*

Unwrapping the Gift of Serenity

1. What makes us persist in trying to change things that won't change?

2. How does *acceptance* lead to the gift of serenity?

3. How does the gift of courage enter into the process of serenity?

4. How is trust a part of the gift of serenity?

12

The Gift of Peace

PERHAPS THE MOST important gift of life recovery is the gift of peace. After all, isn't the absence of peace the reason why so many of us have numbed ourselves through our addictions? We may have felt peaceful temporarily; but then the shame and guilt came, and the peace we so desperately wanted disappeared.

The gift of peace can finally be ours when we have consciously connected with the person of God and with his Son, Jesus Christ. A peaceful heart is only possible when we have made our peace with Jesus, the Prince of Peace. Peace comes when we realize that God is a person with whom we can have a vital connection, not some impersonal force in the universe.

Second, we find the gift of peace when we accept the reality of who we are and can share this reality with others on the same journey of recovery. Those who have received the gift of peace can call themselves an addict or an alcoholic and can share their story comfortably.

Ed was someone who had not yet discovered the gift of peace. Even though he hadn't had a drink in six years, he was what you would call a *dry drunk*. For eighteen years, his wife had pressured him to stop drinking, but it took a warning from his doctor that he would be dead within a year if he didn't stop to finally get him to set aside the bottle. His liver had been in terrible shape, but it recovered. The term *dry drunk* fit Ed to a T, because his state of mind, his moods, and his behaviors were as poisonous to himself and to everyone around him as they had been when he was drinking.

In fact, Janet, his wife, would have said that he was worse than when he was drinking—because at least then she could blame his bad behavior on the booze. Now she didn't know who or what to blame. Ed's moods were totally unpredictable, but they were seldom *up* for any length of time. As soon as anything went wrong, he would blame someone else. The "blame game" was one of his favorite pastimes.

On top of that, he was still impulsive and irresponsible. If he wanted something, he went out and got it right then, regardless of how it would affect anyone else. He didn't think of the consequences of his behavior, just as he hadn't when he was drinking.

A fearless moral inventory was still not part of Ed's repertoire.

At work he was passed over for a promotion that he was convinced he should have gotten. He could understand why he didn't get promoted when he was drinking, but now that he was sober, he blamed his boss and coworkers for holding him back. A fearless moral inventory was still not part of his repertoire.

Ed never had emotional spontaneity with his family—something that Janet longed for. He was cut off from his emotions and was detached relationally from his wife and teenage children. When he retreated into himself, Janet would wonder if he was daydreaming about the "good old days" when he was still drinking.

Janet was confused. She and Ed were both Christians, and she thought their marriage would improve after he stopped drinking. But it seemed to be getting worse. She was hoping that Ed would become more involved with the church and the men's group, but that didn't happen either.

She still walks on eggshells and tries to keep the kids out of Ed's way so they don't set him off. She wonders if Ed resents her because she wanted him to quit drinking. She can't understand why life is still so chaotic and lacking in peace.

The Gift of Peace Defined

Peace is defined as a state of quiet tranquility and as harmony in personal relationships, especially in relationships with God. It is the absence of conflict or violence.

Peace is foreign to the lives of those still caught in their addictions. For someone like Ed, who never took the first step to begin a recovery process, there is little difference between his experience of life in sobriety and his life when he was drinking. Even though he's sober, he has no peace. And the conflict within himself spills over into conflict with those he lives and works with.

The dictionary defines peace, in part, as "freedom from disturbance . . . mental calm . . . freedom from dispute or dissension between individuals or groups."[1] In addition to the *freedom* that seems to accompany peace, it also involves reestablishing friendly relations or becoming reconciled.[2]

One of the most important gifts and promises of life recovery is that it is the path to experiencing God's peace. Jesus told his disciples, just before his arrest, "I am leaving you with a gift— peace of mind and heart. And the peace I give is a gift the world cannot give. So don't be troubled or afraid" (John 14:27). In the Old Testament, the primary word for peace is the familiar Hebrew word *shalom*. Its meaning is broad, relating to peace between people, between nations, and between people and God.

> *In addition to the freedom that seems to accompany peace, it also involves reestablishing friendly relations or becoming reconciled.*

In Isaiah 9:6, the prophet refers to the coming Messiah as the Prince of Peace. Through the death of Jesus Christ and his resurrection, we have peace with God. As the apostle Paul told the Philippians, "Don't worry about anything; instead, pray about everything. Tell God what you need, and thank him for all he has done. Then you will experience God's peace, which exceeds anything we can understand. His peace will guard your hearts and minds as you live in Christ Jesus" (Philippians 4:6-7). In other words, as we seek God's will in our lives and pray with thanksgiving, God's peace will reign in our hearts.

David tells us, "Turn away from evil and do good. Search for peace, and work to maintain it" (Psalm 34:14). In Proverbs, Solomon expands on this idea: "Deceit fills hearts that are plotting evil; joy fills hearts that are planning peace!" (Proverbs 12:20). We must search for, plan for, and work to maintain peace. It is a gift that must be nurtured.

Then there is the promise in Proverbs 14:30: "A peaceful heart leads to a healthy body." A peaceful heart is not filled with stress and anxiety. Both stress and anxiety cause the body to release harmful hormones, which doesn't happen when the heart is peaceful.

So we can say that the gift of peace is both a lack of conflict with others as well as a lack of conflict within ourselves. It is a part of a mature character, which comes from a mature recovery. Mature character stops worldly worry and peacefully regards whatever lies ahead. This gift comes only from time spent living out the Steps and repeatedly turning over to God what is tempting for us to try to control. Our relationships are at rest. The trivial and destructive elements of the world of addiction are no longer able to disrupt our lives.

The gift of peace is founded on a life lived to the fullest and built on our relationship with Christ.

Unlike superficial states of mind, the gift of peace is founded on a life lived to the fullest and built on our relationship with Christ. We are at peace within and without, and each day we find more and more that life is a new gift to be enjoyed. We are filled with gratitude for what is and what may be, and our gratitude stops the nagging regrets of what was and what could have been. God is in control. Love rules our hearts, and our connections with others grow stronger as we live centered in the gift of peace.

The Difference between Peace and Serenity

There is some overlap between the gifts of serenity and peace, but there are also some important differences. Serenity is more of a state of mind. It is internal. Our hearts are calm and tranquil. When we're serene, we're not alarmed by externals. We have learned to accept things as they are; we know when to challenge things that can be changed and when to work for that change. Our souls are at equilibrium.

The gift of peace is also internal, but it has an outward expression. As we experience God's peace, we become at peace with the external world as well. We are at peace with the other people in our lives. Our relationships are healthy and up to date. Nothing needs to be confronted or dealt with. We have no anxieties about our important relationships.

Making Peace versus Keeping the Peace

In the Sermon on the Mount, Jesus says, "God blesses those who work for peace, for they will be called the children of God" (Matthew 5:9). He is referring to peacemakers, people who work to bring harmony and reconciliation. Peacemakers work to bring people into places of agreement.

Peacemakers should not be confused with peace-*keepers*—those who expend their energy trying to keep everybody happy, which is an impossible task. Rather than appeasing others, peacemakers look for common ground and build there.

> *Peacemakers should not be confused with peacekeepers— those who expend their energy trying to keep everybody happy.*

James tells us that "those who are peacemakers will plant seeds of peace and reap a harvest of righteousness" (James 3:18). Peacekeepers seek to calm the emotions in the moment, whereas peacemakers plant seeds of peace that lead to an ongoing harvest.

The Misstep That Robs Us of the Gift of Peace

Ed wanted nothing to do with the Twelve Steps. Not only was he a dry drunk, but he was also a one-stepper— believing that if he simply followed the Bible, he didn't need to work the Twelve Steps. For Ed, "following the Bible" meant going to church, listening to the weekly sermon, and occasionally reading the text for himself— which usually happened only when he was feeling guilty for some hurtful behavior toward his wife or kids.

Ed missed the point of the Twelve Steps on two counts. First, he didn't understand that following the Twelve Steps *is* following the Bible. Life recovery is a path through the Bible designed specifically for those who want to break free from an addiction or problem behavior.

Second, he didn't understand that the word *recovery* is simply a different word for what the Bible calls *sanctification*. If someone asked Ed to define *sanctification*, he would probably say something like this: "It is what we do after we are born again. It's how we grow in our faith." And that would be a good answer.

But if someone asked him to define *recovery*, he would probably respond, "Oh, that's the Twelve Step thing. I don't need that. I haven't had a drink in years. Why would I need recovery?"

Unfortunately, he doesn't seem to understand that recovery is simply what we do after we stop our addictive behavior. It's how we begin to grow again in our lives. Twelve Step recovery is a path of hope, healing, and restoration based on God's truth. It will totally change the way we think and live.

Stopping our addictive behavior is only the beginning. If we never follow through with life recovery, we never leave the starting line. Look at all the gifts of life recovery that Ed never experienced because he refused to work the Steps. He missed out not only on the gifts but also on getting to know the giver of the gifts, God himself. That's the best gift of all.

> *Recovery is simply what we do after we stop our addictive behavior. It's how we begin to grow again in our lives.*

Unwrapping the Gift of Peace

1. How does continuing to live as a "dry drunk" fit into your problem?

2. How is the gift of peace connected to the concept of harmony?

3. If Jesus is the Prince of Peace, how does he bring us peace?

4. What is the difference between "making peace" and "keeping the peace"?

Afterword

AS YOU HAVE SEEN, when we enter into the process called *life recovery*, we become truly gifted. As we faithfully walk the path of recovery, God wants to give us these gifts, not just once but over and over again as needed. We are required only to stay the course. If we slip and fall, we have people around us who help us get up and get back on the right path again.

Along the way in our recovery journey, our giftedness gives us new hope for the future as we are empowered by God and move toward developing good character. We think more clearly now, and as a result we feel more secure. We are no longer controlled by a scarcity mind-set, for we now live out of the abundance of our relationship with God. We are surprised sometimes by our wisdom in situations, our sense of self-control, and how our fearful approach to life has been replaced by the gift of courage. In our developing sense of contentment, we experience true happiness, genuine serenity, and the peace that comes from our relationship with God. These are all gifts coming to us from God's grace and love for us.

As we have worked through understanding these twelve gifts, it has become clear that, when people "just stop" in their recovery, they miss out on all these gifts. They miss out on these good things from God. That's why we so strongly urge everyone in need to begin the recovery journey. It's called *life* recovery for a reason. Who among us hasn't had issues to face that come just from living life? Recovery is simply a way to describe the process of resolving the issues of life. Why would anyone resist the process of recovery?

Whenever you struggle with staying on the path of recovery, remember the twelve gifts of life recovery that God desires to give to you. They are not earned—they are God's gifts. Our part—the effort we make—comes as we seek to expand each gift into more areas of our lives, so that we are daily "growing in every way more and more like Christ" (Ephesians 4:15).

As you begin to experience the gifts of life recovery, we would love to hear from you:

Stephen Arterburn
SArterburn@newlife.com

David Stoop
DrStoop@cox.net

Appendix

An Introduction to Life Recovery

IN 1990, we partnered with Tyndale House Publishers to create *The Life Recovery Bible*, a unique combination of a study Bible and a devotional Bible, for fellow strugglers who were involved in Twelve Step recovery programs and wanted to integrate the Twelve Steps with the Bible. We had studied the Oxford Group movement, which essentially birthed Alcoholics Anonymous. Both Bill W. and Dr. Bob, the originators of the Twelve Steps, were deeply involved in those groups. They were living out the four Oxford Group Absolutes of *absolute honesty*, *absolute purity*, *absolute unselfishness*, and *absolute love* as they helped others find the sobriety they were experiencing.

In the beginning, there were no Twelve Steps. The Twelve Steps of Alcoholics Anonymous eventually emerged from hours of discussions between Dr. Bob and Bill W., from studying portions of the Bible that supported their Oxford Group experiences, and from their own recovery experiences.

The three portions of Scripture specifically identified as foundational in the development of the Twelve Steps were the Sermon on the Mount (which includes the Beatitudes); the book of James (which focuses on several Twelve Step fundamentals, such as *confession*); and 1 Corinthians 13 (also known as "the love chapter"). All three of these portions of Scripture from the New Testament clearly establish the Christian and biblical roots of Alcoholics Anonymous and the Twelve Steps.

In the early days of AA, when conservative Christian values and truths were unapologetically used to help others in recovery, the success rate was quite amazing. One documented study revealed that 93 percent of the people in a group in Ohio never relapsed. For a problem that had resulted in hopelessness and helplessness for centuries, this was truly amazing. Even more amazing is how long it has taken to establish a movement back to those original Christian truths and values. That is the purpose of *The Life Recovery Bible* and other resources that accompany it, including the newest publications: *The Twelve Gifts of Life Recovery* and *The Twelve Laws of Life Recovery*.

Where Are You?

We have found that people come to these materials from very different places and with varied expectations. You may be someone who has been in recovery for a while and wants to integrate biblical wisdom into all aspects of your recovery. Maybe you've come to understand what it takes to get better, and now you want more insight into the *how* and *why* of the changes you have experienced. With *The Twelve Gifts of Life Recovery* and its companion text, *The Twelve Laws of Life Recovery*, not only will you gain a better understanding of the Life Recovery process, but you will also be guided toward a more intimate relationship with God and will become much more effective in helping others.

Perhaps you are brand new to the concept of recovery, and you've begun to work the Steps in a Christian group, such as a Life Recovery group. The Life Recovery materials will strengthen your recovery and keep your focus on Jesus as your higher power. As you experience this with other believers, or with those still searching for what to believe, you will most likely find this material a unique, proven, and effective way to live a Christian life that grows deeper and produces richer results in all areas.

You also might be a person who is just curious about Life Recovery. *Does it complement or conflict with AA? Can I use these principles if I'm not an addict? Are they necessary, or can I just take one step to believe in Jesus as Savior?* If you are curious, you are looking in the right place. When you see others totally transform their lives, it will validate the power of Life Recovery. When you follow these Steps and incorporate these materials into your life, the transformation you will experience will allow you to live with a peace and freedom that too few ever experience.

Individual Use of Life Recovery Materials

There are many ways to use the Life Recovery materials to strengthen your recovery and prevent a relapse. One way is to start with *The Life Recovery Bible*. Interspersed throughout the text of the Bible are devotionals, profiles, and articles about recovery principles that you will find helpful in your recovery. Based on feedback we've received over the years, the features that will likely come to mean the most to you are the notes at the bottom of each page that help you understand and apply the Bible verses you are reading.

Starting your day with a chapter from the Bible and the notes that go along with it will focus your attention on God's truth and on your commitment not only to *stop* something that has become a problem but also to *start* something that is healing and transformative. A few additional moments of reading from *The Life Recovery Devotional*, followed by the Serenity Prayer (or an original prayer), will connect you with God and provide inspiration for the rest of your day.

In beginning your journey of life recovery, the best tool may be *The Life Recovery Workbook*, which covers all Twelve Steps. You can take one Step a day, a week, or a month. The pace is up to you, but in the workbook you will find new insights into yourself as you work out the answers to the questions there. When you have finished the workbook, you can move into *The Life Recovery Journey*, which provides four Bible studies for each step. Working through *The Life Recovery Journey*, you will find both Twelve Step concepts and biblical truth in all of the recovery principles. You'll learn what it means to *work the Steps*, rather than just knowing about them or reading them. Working the Steps unleashes God's power through his truth.

When you are ready (which may be at any time along the way), *The Twelve Laws of Life Recovery* will show you some requirements that you must meet in order to develop the life you've always wanted, and *The Twelve Gifts of Life Recovery* will unwrap the gifts that arise from adhering to the Steps in every area of your life.

Just as you started your day with *The Life Recovery Bible* and *The Life Recovery Devotional*, you might consider ending your day with *The Life Recovery Journal*. With it, you can express your feelings about where you are on the journey and document your progress by putting on paper what emerges as the most important developments in your recovery and transformation. If you use these materials in this way, you will develop spiritually, mature emotionally, grow relationally, and experience Christ-centered sobriety and serenity.

Group Power

What you can accomplish on your own is exponentially magnified when you become involved in a Life Recovery group. You can find out if there's a group in your area by calling 1-800-NEW-LIFE (1-800-639-5433). If one does not exist, that same number will lead you to materials and methods to help you start your own group. Or you can go to www.liferecovery bible.com and download the reproducible flyers that tell people about the group. Ask your church leaders for permission, a place, and a time to lead the meeting yourself. A smartphone or other media device will allow you to start each meeting with video material. We have created video material, which you can use to start a group, in support of every Step, Law, and Gift. You don't have to come up with anything new. We have provided the materials for you to get started.

After viewing the video clip you've chosen, simply be there to facilitate the discussion. Don't allow anyone to dominate the group, criticize, or try to fix someone else. These guidelines, as well as a procedure for starting a group, can also be downloaded at www .liferecoverybible.com.

One of the best ways to go through the material as a group is to work on the Step that corresponds with the month of the year. So January, for example, would be the month to focus on Step One. *The Life Recovery Bible* and *The Life Recovery Journey* are set up to study the Steps in this way. *The Book of Life Recovery* provides four Bible studies for each step, allowing the group to study the same material during the week, discuss it, and share their own struggles. With the addition of *The Twelve Laws of Life Recovery* and *The Twelve Gifts of Life Recovery*, a portion of the meeting can be reserved for someone to present a newly developed or newly understood principle derived from those resources.

Anytime you need support or direction for your group, or if you encounter difficulty in leading a group, you can contact a Life Recovery specialist at 1-800-NEW-LIFE. Even if you're fairly new to the recovery process, you can jump in and start a new group. With all of the resources we've developed, we've tried to keep it simple, accessible, and practical.

Notes

CHAPTER 1: THE GIFT OF HOPE

1. *Merriam-Webster's 11th Collegiate Dictionary*, version 3.0, copyright © 2003 by Merriam-Webster, Inc.

CHAPTER 3: THE GIFT OF CHARACTER

1. *Oxford Dictionaries*, copyright © 2015 Oxford University Press; www.oxforddictionaries.com/us/definition/american_english /character.
2. *Recollected Words of Abraham Lincoln*, compiled and edited by Don E. Fehrenbacher and Virginia Fehrenbacher (Stanford, CA: Stanford University Press, 1996), 43.

CHAPTER 5: THE GIFT OF SECURITY

1. *Oxford Dictionaries*, copyright © 2015 Oxford University Press; www.oxforddictionaries.com/us/definition/american_english /security.

CHAPTER 6: THE GIFT OF ABUNDANCE

1. Ibid.; www.oxforddictionaries.com/us/definition/american _english/abundance?searchDictCode=all.

CHAPTER 7: THE GIFT OF WISDOM

1. Cheryl Eckl, "If You Would Be Wise: Some Tips for Finding Wisdom," Living on the Razor's Edge blog, July 23, 2014; www .psychologytoday.com/blog/living-the-razors-edge/201407/if -you-would-be-wise.

CHAPTER 8: THE GIFT OF SELF-CONTROL

1. *Oxford Dictionaries*, copyright © 2015 Oxford University Press; http://www.oxforddictionaries.com/definition/english/self -control?searchDictCode=all.

CHAPTER 9: THE GIFT OF COURAGE

1. Ibid.; www.oxforddictionaries.com/us/definition/american _english/courage.
2. "Nelson Mandela: in his own words," *The Telegraph*, December 6, 2013; www.telegraph.co.uk/news/worldnews/nelson-mandela /9734032/Nelson-Mandela-in-his-own-words.html.

CHAPTER 10: THE GIFT OF HAPPINESS

1. *Oxford Dictionaries*, copyright © 2015 Oxford University Press; www.oxforddictionaries.com/us/definition/american_english /happy.

CHAPTER 11: THE GIFT OF SERENITY

1. For a complete text of the original Serenity Prayer, see www .beliefnet.com/Prayers/Protestant/Addiction/Serenity-Prayer .aspx.

CHAPTER 12: THE GIFT OF PEACE

1. *Oxford Dictionaries*, copyright © 2015 Oxford University Press; www.oxforddictionaries.com/us/definition/american_english /peace.
2. Ibid.

About the Authors

STEPHEN ARTERBURN is the founder and chairman of New Life Ministries—the nation's largest faith-based broadcast, counseling, and treatment ministry—and is the host of the nationally syndicated *New Life Live!* daily radio program, which airs on more than 180 radio stations nationwide, on Sirius XM radio, and on television. Steve is also the founder of the Women of Faith conferences, attended by more than 4 million women, and of HisMatchforMe.com. Steve is a nationally known public speaker and has been featured in national media venues such as *Oprah*, *Inside Edition*, *Good Morning America*, *CNN Live*, the *New York Times*, *USA Today*, and *US News & World Report*. In August 2000, Steve was inducted into the National Speakers Association's Hall of Fame.

A bestselling author, Steve has written more than one hundred books, including the popular Every Man's series. He is a Gold Medallion–winning author and has been nominated for numerous other writing awards.

Steve has degrees from Baylor University and the University of North Texas, as well as two honorary doctorate degrees. Steve resides with his family in Indiana.

DAVID STOOP, PhD, is a licensed clinical psychologist who received a master's in theology from Fuller Theological Seminary and a doctorate from the University of Southern California. He is a co-host on the *New Life Live!* radio and TV program. David is the founder and director of the Center for Family Therapy in Newport Beach, California. He is also an adjunct professor at Fuller Seminary and serves on the executive board of the American Association of Christian Counselors. David is a Gold Medallion–winning author who has has written more than thirty books, including *Forgiving the Unforgivable* and *You Are What You Think*. He resides with his wife, Jan, in Newport Beach, California.

BLESSINGS AND WISDOM
FOR YOUR LIFE RECOVERY JOURNEY

978-1-4964-0269-1   978-1-4964-0270-7

From the creators of the bestselling Life Recovery series, *The Twelve Gifts of Life Recovery* and *The Twelve Laws of Life Recovery* illuminate the wisdom and gifts that God imparts as you travel through the Twelve Steps of Life Recovery.

With expert insight and biblical truth, recovery pioneers Stephen Arterburn and David Stoop explore the life recovery "laws" that God honors, as well as the blessings for those who seek him. These powerful books reveal God's faithfulness in your everyday walk, enriching your life in ways you've never imagined as you invite him to work within you.

————————————

Find out more at **LifeRecoveryBible.com.**

Find Healing in God's Word Every Day.

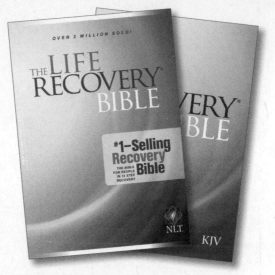

Celebrating over 2 million copies sold!

The Life Recovery Bible is today's bestselling Bible for people in recovery. In the accurate and easy-to-understand New Living Translation, *The Life Recovery Bible* leads people to the true source of healing—God himself. Special features created by two of today's leading recovery experts—David Stoop, Ph.D., and Stephen Arterburn, M.Ed.—include the following:

Recovery Study Notes: Thousands of Recovery-themed notes interspersed throughout the Bible pinpoint passages and thoughts important to recovery.

Twelve Step Devotionals: A reading chain of 84 Bible-based devotionals tied to the Twelve Steps of recovery.

Serenity Prayer Devotionals: Based on the Serenity Prayer, these 29 devotionals are placed next to the verses from which they are drawn.

Recovery Principle Devotionals: Bible-based devotionals, arranged topically, are a guide to key recovery principles.

Find *The Life Recovery Bible* at your local Christian bookstore or wherever books are sold. Learn more at www.LifeRecoveryBible.com.

Available editions:
NLT Hardcover 978-1-4143-0962-0
NLT Softcover 978-1-4143-0961-3
Personal Size Softcover 978-1-4143-1626-0
Large Print Hardcover 978-1-4143-9856-3

Large Print Softcover 978-1-4143-9857-0
KJV Hardcover 978-1-4143-8150-3
KJV Softcover 978-1-4143-8506-8

CP0107

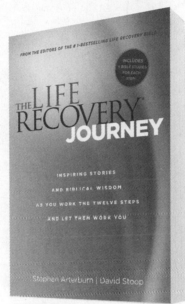

Check out these great resources to help you on your path to recovery:

The Life Recovery Journal has been carefully created to guide you through the recovery process. The questions and quotes will help you to write honest reflections, reinforce what you're learning, and give insight into your recovery as a whole person.

The Life Recovery Workbook is about transformation: from death to life, from addiction to recovery. As you work through each of the Twelve Steps, the challenging spiritual lessons will strengthen you to live free from addiction.

The easy-to-read, down-to-earth meditations in *The Life Recovery Devotional* are designed to help you find the recovery, rest, and peace that Jesus promises. They will help you understand the struggles we all face— in recovery, in overcoming temptation, and in getting back on track after a relapse.